Other Books by Stephen R. Graves and Thomas G. Addington

*Behind the Bottom Line: Powering Business
Life with Spiritual Wisdom*

*Life@Work on Leadership: Enduring Insights
for Men and Women of Faith*

Daily Focus: Daily Readings for Integrating Faith in the Workplace

The Building Block Series

Framing Your Ambition
The Hard Work of Rest
Cornerstones for Calling
Ethical Anchors
The Mentoring Blueprint

The Fourth Frontier: Exploring the New World of Work

The Cornerstones for Life at Work
A Case for Character
A Case for Skill
A Case for Calling
A Case for Serving

CLOUT

CLOUT

TAPPING SPIRITUAL WISDOM

to BECOME

a PERSON *of* INFLUENCE

Stephen R. Graves | Thomas G. Addington

Foreword by John C. Maxwell

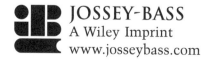

JOSSEY-BASS
A Wiley Imprint
www.josseybass.com

Published by Jossey-Bass
A Wiley Imprint
989 Market Street, San Francisco, CA 94103-1741   www.josseybass.com

Jossey-Bass books and products are available through most bookstores. To contact Jossey-Bass directly call our Customer Care Department within the U.S. at 800-956-7739, outside the U.S. at 317-572-3986 or fax 317-572-4002.

Jossey-Bass also publishes its books in a variety of electronic formats. Some content that appears in print may not be available in electronic books.

Unless otherwise noted in the text, Scripture quotations are from The HOLY BIBLE: New International Version, copyright © 1973, 1978, 1984. Used by permission of Zondervan Bible Publishers.

Library of Congress Cataloging-in-Publication Data

Graves, Stephen R., date.
   Clout: tapping spiritual wisdom to become a person of influence /
Stephen R. Graves and Thomas G. Addington; foreword by John C. Maxwell.
      p. cm.
Includes bibliographical references and index.
      ISBN 0-7879-6475-1 (alk. paper)
      1. Influence (Psychology)—Religious aspects—Christianity. I.
Addington, Thomas G., date. II. Title.
   BV4597.53.I52G73 2003
   248.4—dc21
                                                                2002155905

Printed in the United States of America

FIRST EDITION
HB Printing   10 9 8 7 6 5 4 3 2

Contents

     Jesus on Influence

8   **Mentoring**   103
     Strategic Life Coaching

9   **Breaking the Genetic Code on Influence**   117
     Universal Models of Applying Influence

10   **Influence Has an Org Chart**   131
     Understanding the Four Spheres of Influence

11   **When Influence Becomes Influenza**   145
     Influence Gone Bad

12   **Class-Seven Influence**   161
     10,585 Days and Counting

     References   175

     The Authors   177

     About Cornerstone Group   179

     Index   181

Foreword

As an author and speaker, I have spent years communicating the value of effective leadership to people in all arenas of life. In my own experience and by studying the experiences of others, I have found that everything rises and falls on leadership. And leadership is influence or, as my friends Steve and Tom call it, *clout*. And how we develop and use that clout is up to us.

We all have our own clout bank account. We build it, we spend it, we borrow on it, we loan against it, we lose it, we squander it, we hoard it, we try to rebuild it, we share it, we invest it. But at the end of the day, it is ours—to use or to abuse. Consequently, we should see our clout as a very real asset that we must steward.

Clout is something we all want more of. And we all want to do a better job exercising the clout we have. The good news, according to Steve and Tom, is that clout is something we can all build. No one is stuck with a bank account that cannot grow. But then, no one is guaranteed to keep the bank account they currently have. It must be worked and reworked with the care and attention we give to our life savings.

Our clout is the core of our personal influence. It can be used correctly for exciting and fulfilling results, or it can be used wrongly for disappointing and nagging results. It can be rooted in a source bigger than ourselves, which is wisdom, or it can be homespun and tied down by a "me only" perspective. It can be maximized with a few tools, and it can be customized with a few tips.

Right off the bat, Steve and Tom help us to distinguish the difference in the right kind of clout and the wrong kind of clout, which is really the baseline for the conversation on influence. Every segment and every crevice of our society can use more of the right kind of clout. Especially now.

People expressing the right kind of clout is exactly what Jesus had in mind when he talked about people being salt and light. It is also what Aristotle called the persuasion triangle.

Steve and Tom have provided a personal book full of fun stories and ready-to-apply guidance. *Clout* is for anyone hoping to better understand and improve their personal influence. It is timely, and it has the potential to change your life. Don't miss a page.

March 2003

John C. Maxwell
Founder, The INJOY Group

Acknowledgments

Thank you, Kristi Reimer. Though you're becoming commonplace in our publishing endeavors, it is still fun watching you stretch your already accomplished writing muscles.

Thank you, Dick Parker. Your willingness to jump in at the last minute and help us heave this project across the finish line is greatly appreciated.

Thank you, Sheryl Fullerton and the entire Jossey-Bass team. When our sails hung flat and limp on this book, you provided the gust of encouragement and enthusiasm we needed to help us finish the race.

Thank you, Chip MacGregor. Every project we do seems to reveal more of your goodness.

To Fellowship Bible Church of Northwest Arkansas:

We are privileged to enjoy a world-class influence incubator in our own backyard. For the last fifteen years we have watched you recruit, build, and release hundreds upon hundreds of class-seven influencers.

Robert, Gary, Mickey, Sam, Chip, and the rest of the team: you have the right kind of clout.

CLOUT

An Extra Dose of Vitamin I

Expanding Your Personal Influence

The entire ocean is affected by a single pebble.

—Blaise Pascal

NOT LONG AGO, I WAS INVITED TO A PARTY unlike any I had ever attended. Intrigued, I accepted the invitation and made my way to the site of the festivities on the designated date.

A number of other men and I had been summoned to a local eatery with a menu featuring big steaks for big men and a decor that could best be described as Modern Testosterone. We were there to celebrate a young man's thirteenth birthday. I was quite certain a thirteen-year-old's birthday party had never been held here before, but that's precisely why this venue was chosen. It wasn't a kids' pizza joint; it was a man's place.

After we completed the steak dinner, the sense of fun and laughter began to shift toward solemnity. Anticipating what lay ahead in the evening's activities, all the men at the table grew a little nervous. None of us had ever been part of an event quite like this, and we all were curious to see how it would come together and how each part would fit in.

Austin, the young guest of honor, sat at the end of the table, looking anxious and a little awkward as the center of so much attention. But he was also eager to know what was coming. Everyone at the table was somehow connected to him. There were coaches, teachers, friends, fathers of friends, friends of his father's, relatives, and other men who had played an important role in the boy's life.

One by one, each guest addressed Austin. They told stories from his past and shared snapshots of his character—the way he befriended and protected kids who had a hard time fitting in at school, his encouragement of his basketball teammates, his humility when he succeeded academically, his quick and easy sense of humor, his courage, and his faith. They also offered advice about how Austin could further cultivate those qualities and become a man of integrity and strength.

At the end of the evening, despite the manly atmosphere, you would have had a hard time finding an eye that wasn't sparkling with tears. It was a fun and yet moving evening for all of us. It's also a safe assumption that the night will be indelibly etched in Austin's memory until his old age. At least that was the intention.

The mastermind of this event was my friend John, Austin's father. He had asked every man who shared a positive relationship with Austin to communicate something meaningful that would serve his son well as he entered adulthood. Together we built a rite of passage for Austin, a bridge for him to cross into manhood.

It was a powerful experience that will stay with me for a long time. It's also a great illustration of a subject we've been thinking about for quite some time: the idea of personal influence.

As a father, John was deliberately and intentionally trying to influence his son and affect the direction of the boy's life. The event required forethought, planning, and ingenuity, and John went to great lengths in an attempt to bring about a certain outcome: the dream that his son would grow up to be a certain kind of man.

Are there any guarantees that John will see his dreams for his son realized? Absolutely not. Although he has done and will continue to do everything within his power to influence Austin to make wise decisions and walk down certain paths, he cannot force things to happen the way he wants them to. As parents, we can point our children in the right direction, but they have to walk the journey. Other people, events, circumstances, and choices will affect Austin's life, and over them John has no control. Some may cause him grief; others may exceed his wildest expectations.

Influence, by definition, can shape, but it cannot guarantee.

The same week as Austin's birthday and manhood celebration, another friend, Mark, called and asked to talk. Over a Coke, he relayed a heartbreaking story. He had just returned from a trip to Georgia to bury his father. Mark's dad had divorced a long time ago and never remarried. At the end of his life, he was sick and living alone—truly alone. No friends or family nearby, no interaction with neighbors, no community at all. Fighting for control but with his voice breaking, Mark told me that no one had come to his father's funeral—not even a minister. Think about that for a minute. It was a funeral where not one friend came to say thanks, or that you did a good job with your life. A funeral where not one family member came to pay last respects. Not one official came out of a sense of obligation. The elderly gentleman, whether by choice or circumstance, had spent his final years, months, days, and minutes without the comforting presence of someone who truly cared. Mark was enveloped in grief.

I struggled to come up with a way to comfort my friend, but my own heart was aching. As we sat there with our forgotten drinks, I was struck by the brutal reality that life often doesn't end as we hope it will. Many of our early dreams are unrealized at best, and shattered at worst. All the maneuvering and planning we can muster cannot guarantee the outcomes we so desperately desire.

VITAMIN I

We hear a lot these days about the importance of good nutrition. Vitamins and supplements nearly tumble off the grocery store and pharmacy shelf. Newspapers and magazines are jammed with articles about recent studies promising that vitamin X will help our hearts, ease our pain, vanquish disease-causing molecules, trim our waistlines, regrow our hair, repel summer mosquitoes, reduce stress, or—well, you can fill in the blank. Many of us are beefing up our intake of vitamins A, B, C, E, and so on, down the alphabet in the hope that it will pay off with good health and a high-quality life.

Vitamins are unquestionably important for the well being of our body. But do we focus as much on the less tangible aspects of our lives—

our character, our spirit, our soul—as we do on our physical health? Are we doing anything to evaluate and enhance our impact on the world around us?

What if a new product hit the shelves tomorrow at the local supermarket—a supplement that would increase not our physical well-being but our ability to *influence*? This product would be called vitamin I, and it would enable us to deliver a greater impact on people, events, and outcomes in any job or relationship. Would it sell out? You bet it would. There might not be a more universal appetite than that for influence. What mom doesn't want to have more effective influence on her daughter? What coach doesn't want to shape his players, win more games, and graduate better kids? No matter our walk of life, most of us desire to leave a positive footprint of influence. A mayor hopes to influence her town. A pastor hopes to influence his flock. A teacher hopes to influence his students. A physician hopes to influence her patients. A consultant hopes to influence his clients. A boss hopes to influence her employees. The list goes on and on.

We believe that most people have the potential to achieve a greater level of personal influence. What we offer in this book is not a pill or a magic bullet that suddenly expands your influence to new heights without any effort. Growth in any area requires calories. What this book does contain is our analysis, observations, and insights about influence, filtered against the best historical wisdom, contemporary thinking, and real-life examples that we could find. That's what we present to you; that's our vitamin I.

Defining Influence Correctly

Influence is a powerful force in our society; whole industries have developed around it. The lobbying industry tries to influence the government according to the best interests of those they represent. Advertisers try to persuade consumers to spend their money on certain products or services. Sales and marketing teams spend enormous resources trying to make the business deal that will benefit their company. Politicians wield nationwide telemarketing campaigns hoping to sway last-minute voters. Parents are invited to an evening seminar promising better results with their children. Everywhere we look, we can see influence at work.

I saw it just the other night when the doorbell rang as we were finishing dinner. It was an unusual evening because all the family members were present and accounted for at the table. At the front door was a good-looking high school sophomore proudly wearing a new football jersey. Our entire family crowded around the front door, which pushed my two teenage daughters slightly out of their comfort zone (translation: they were ready to die from embarrassment). The football player was selling a coupon packet to benefit the athletic booster club. I arrived halfway through the pitch. This kid definitely had a future in sales. For about three minutes, I listened to a persuasive case as to why I should transfer a ten-dollar bill from my wallet to his in exchange for a coupon book. It worked. Effective influence usually does, even at an elementary level.

Unfortunately, most of us don't give influence much thought until an element of personal gain is at stake, or something or someone has fallen in the ditch. Then we scour bookstores and search the Web for insider tips to close the deal, make the friend, achieve the promotion, get the advantage, fix the broken relationship, or improve the circumstance. When we're on the hunt for fast-acting vitamin I so we can become influential quickly, the process is often self-motivated and self-interested.

Our approach in this book is different. We believe influence is much bigger—and purer—than a tool to wield against the world to get things for ourselves. We define influence as *a person's ability to shape people and mold outcomes.* This is influence in the raw. The process may not happen immediately, or even within the influencer's lifetime, but at some point things turn out differently than they would have because one person brought himself to bear on the situation.

Clout Versus Influence

The title of this book is *Clout: Tapping Spiritual Wisdom to Become a Person of Influence.* We want to spend some time thinking about these terms.

First of all, the dictionary defines *clout* as "a blow with the fist," "a long, powerful hit in baseball," "power or muscle," and "influence or pull." Obviously, we're primarily concerned here with that final definition. But the others are significant as well. Wrapped up in the idea of clout is something very strong, muscular, direct, and intentional. It's a short word that packs a lot of punch—literally, since one of the definitions is synonymous with a left front hook.

Looking at how the term is used in the media reveals further insights:

- Clout involves status, prestige, authority, and power.
- With clout, there's often an element of intimidation or pulling strings.
- People are often forced to defer to someone with clout, even if they don't want to.
- Many people prefer clout over effective performance.
- One writer referred to people with clout as having "the keys to the bulldozer," such that they can roll over barriers.
- Clout is related to experience and "persuasive muscle."

You may be noticing some rather ugly connotations associated with the idea of clout; if you're not sold on the concept yet, bear with us a moment. First let's look at the word *influence,* and then we'll come back to clout.

Dictionary definitions for *influence* include "a power indirectly or intangibly affecting a person or course of events," and "to cause a change in the character, thought, or action of; to have an effect upon." A less common meaning is "an occult ethereal fluid believed to flow from the stars and to affect the fate of men." This may be somewhat startling and sound rather bizarre, but it reflects the fact that influence is a mysterious, intangible, almost mystical process that doesn't depend on status or prestige but rather on character, careful decision making, and—quite often—circumstances beyond our control. The word comes from the Latin verb *influere,* meaning to flow in, and this is exactly what happens in the influence process: one person "flows in" to a set of circumstances or the life of another individual.

So, where does that leave us? The word *clout* is related to hitting someone on the head or flexing muscle. The word *influence* involves an intangible, even ethereal process of producing change. Someone with influence flows; someone with clout bulldozes. Are the two ideas mutually exclusive?

Not at all. We think that clout and influence are two sides of the same coin. Part of being influential is having clout: the direct, authoritative, cut-through-the-red-tape attitude and position necessary to produce results. Part of it is more shadowy and indirect, less clearly understood. Proper understanding of influence involves acceptance of both ideas. True, there are negative connotations on both sides: intimidation and hunger for power with clout, sneakiness and manipulation with influence. But part of our goal is to reshape some of these preconceptions for the better and to merge the appropriate and worthy elements of both ideas into a new, healthy outlook on personal influence. In this book, we package the terms *clout* and *influence* together for one central message. Stay with us as we develop the idea.

INFLUENCE *and* LEADERSHIP

By now you might have a question in mind: What's the difference between leadership and influence? Is this just another book about leadership disguised in different terminology?

It's a legitimate question, and the short answer is no. Leadership and influence are certainly related and do often overlap—great leaders can wield tremendous influence, and people of influence often occupy a leadership position. But by nature they are two separate entities.

To start with, leadership is tangible and contained. It is usually a conscious mind-set, a prescribed and clearly defined role limited to a certain situation that a person accepts for a period of time or season of life. Leadership is most often carried out in public and is openly discussed among followers and observers. There is usually a cause-and-effect relationship between a leader's words and actions and the events that immediately follow (though the results may or may not be long-term). Leaders act on people.

Influence is a much bigger picture, one that is harder to draw. If leadership is the part of the iceberg we see floating above the surface, influence is the giant mass lurking below, out of sight. It is often unconscious; a person may exert influence without being aware of it, just as one may be influenced without knowing it. Influence is subtle, hidden, and shadowy. It is mysterious; it often takes place behind the scenes. Influence does not depend on a person's education, position, or financial situation, and it crosses lines of culture and ethnicity. A person's influence may not be directly felt or cause immediate results, but when it does find a target, the effect is usually broad and widespread. Influencers act on people *and* outcomes.

Leadership lends itself to formulaic duplication; influence is much more difficult to identify and analyze. A leader says, "I lead the charge"; an influencer says, "I shape the outcome." Our culture is captivated by leadership but driven by influence.

Karl Marx, for example, was not a leader during his lifetime, even though he wrote the *Communist Manifesto* and other works. He was an obscure, poor German whose ideas about religion, capitalism, injustice, and suffering made barely a ripple on world consciousness. When he died on March 17, 1883, only eleven people attended his funeral. At the time, Frederic Engels, a contemporary who shared many of his political ideas, said Marx's name and work would endure through the ages; it seemed an unlikely boast at the time. But with the upheaval and unrest produced by the Industrial Revolution, Marx's influence rolled out in waves that ultimately toppled governments and shook societies. Looking back at the twentieth century, with the spread of communism and its effects on the globe, Engels's remarks seem like an understatement.

The former CEO of GE, Jack Welch, was a leader; Federal Reserve Bank Chairman Alan Greenspan is an influencer. Leadership is the surface; influence is the current.

Here's a summary of some of the differences between leadership and influence:

- Leadership is visible; influence is out of sight.
- Leadership is usually conscious; influence is often unconscious.
- Leadership is contained; influence crosses boundaries.
- Leadership is immediate; influence is long-term.
- Leadership is public; influence is often behind-the-scenes.
- Leadership is formulaic; influence is mysterious.
- Leadership captivates culture; influence drives culture.

In presenting these differences, we don't want to falsely elevate influence over leadership, but we do want to make the case that influence is bigger, deeper, and a more difficult skill to cultivate than leadership. If we had to choose between whether we wanted to exert leadership or influence, we would choose influence.

KINDS *of* PEOPLE

When it comes to influence, people generally fall into one of eight categories.

1.   PEOPLE WHO HAVE LESS CLOUT THAN THEY THINK THEY DO

We all know individuals who think they're more powerful, important, and interesting than they really are. You may have found yourself talking to someone like this at a social occasion and begun looking for a way to escape the conversation. Often these people gravitate toward the spotlight and look for any chance to sound off about themselves. But in the end, they're just a lot of noise and flash, and they rarely make a substantial impact on anyone or any situation. They are, in the words of a Texas buddy of mine, "all hat, no cattle."

2.   PEOPLE WHO HAVE MORE CLOUT THAN THEY THINK THEY DO

Most people fall into this category because they are barely tapping the influence potential they possess. It's as if they're perched within reach of the peak of a mountain, and a small push would allow them to crest the summit and fly down the other side, gaining more momentum and speed in their influence ability than they ever thought possible. But even though these individuals are capable of having a greater impact than they already do, they are still exerting enormous influence in their normal pattern of life and in a natural way. They just don't know it.

3.   PEOPLE WHO ARE UNDERAPPLYING THEIR CLOUT

Some people deliberately avoid being influential. These individuals are often enormously and obviously talented, but for some reason (lack of confidence, laziness, rebellion) they refuse to live up to what is expected of them. They might possess great physical or mental ability. They might be gifted socially or spiritually. They might have wealth, title, or personality. Whatever it is, we expect them to cast a greater shadow of influence than they do. Perhaps Jesus had these people in mind when He warned, "From everyone who has been given much, much will be demanded; and from the one who has been entrusted with much, much more will be asked" (Luke 12:48; all biblical citations are from the *New International Version*).

4. PEOPLE WHO ARE WRONGLY APPLYING THEIR CLOUT

We don't need to be told about the dark side of influence. History is full of notorious characters—Adolf Hitler, Idi Amin, Jim Jones—who used their considerable persuasive abilities for the destruction of humanity. Many of us have witnessed influence gone bad firsthand. It's ugly when it happens, and it often produces more ugliness. A current example is the ever-growing rap sheet of corporate executives who have inflated earnings to line their own coffers, usually at the expense of shareholders and employee retirement funds. The scandal that started with Enron has spiraled outward to include as many as twenty companies at last count, and it is still growing. This epidemic is a testament to the temptation to abuse power and influence for personal gain.

5. PEOPLE WHO HAVE CLOUT IN ONE AREA
   BUT FEEL POWERLESS IN ANOTHER

It's not uncommon for someone to have a certain part of life in great shape but to feel like a total failure in another. This discrepancy often occurs between public and private life. A woman may be highly respected and extremely capable at work, but her kids are out of control, her husband has filed for divorce, and she doesn't know how to fix the shambles of her home life. Although this scenario is common, the reverse can also be true. A man may be a great husband and father, but at the office doubt, insecurity, and a sense of incompetence plague him. Too often, these people can't seem to transfer the principles of influence that work so well in one arena of life to another set of circumstances and relationships with a successful result.

6. PEOPLE WHO ARE REFLECTING ON THE TRANSFER
   AND SUSTAINABILITY OF THEIR CLOUT

In our consulting practice, we have worked with many executives who are reaching the end of their career and anticipating a transition or succession of some kind. One such leader was the first-generation founder of his company. He had built it into a $200 million business, and it was time for him to get off the horse and let someone else ride it through the next season of growth. He knew it was time, the board knew it, his executive team knew it—even key customers knew he needed to pass the reins. He wasn't running the business into the ground by any means, but he was growing short on energy and entering a new season of life, which meant a different role in the company.

We developed several plans, but whenever it came time to pull the trigger, this gentleman couldn't go through with the transition. As we continued to work with him, we realized that he was gripped by fear regarding the sustainability of his influence. The question of how he would be remembered, whether his twenty-five-year legacy would crumble or continue, absolutely paralyzed him. Once we realized what was driving his fear, we were able to coach this CEO and president through a transition that helped ensure the continuation of key elements of his influence in the direction of the company.

7. PEOPLE AT THE SUNRISE OF THEIR LIFE OR CAREER
   WHO ARE BUILDING THEIR CLOUT

Recently I spoke to a gathering of young up-and-comers in the Silicon Valley area. There were about three hundred young men and women in attendance, with dazzling professional pedigrees. After my thirty-minute presentation, I spent another hour and a half talking to these folks individually and in small groups. I realized that the common muscle being flexed that evening was the clout muscle. Almost every single attendee wanted to take his or her influence to the next level. Early in their professional lives, they were hungry for greater influence; they wanted to make deposits into their clout bank account. What I emphasized with them, and what we want to stress here, is that there are appropriate and inappropriate ways to achieve clout. A desire for influence can sometimes cloud our judgment, and if we stoop to a strategy that compromises our integrity, we risk losing the esteem of others and our own self-respect.

8. PEOPLE WHO QUESTION WHETHER A DIRTY WORD LIKE CLOUT
   CAN BE LINKED WITH PURE SPIRITUAL MATTERS

We acknowledge that the concepts of clout and influence have a dark side hinting at corruption, manipulation, and intimidation.

Because of this dark side, many people who are trying to build a good and pure life assume that they shouldn't strive in this area, that influence is not an appropriate tool for spiritual edification. Obviously, we don't think this is true, and we hope to clear up the misconception in the next section (and throughout this book).

Each category deserves some attention and gets it in the following chapters. But one thing is certain: the topic of influence applies to everyone, regardless of personality, circumstance, age, or role in life. The call to be influential in a positive way is an inherent part of what it means to be human.

Wouldn't you agree that there's something inside all of us that periodically brings us up short such that we ask, "Why was I put here on this earth? What am I doing? Will my life make a difference? Am I really using my resources in a significant way?" We may ignore or even run from these questions for a time, even for years, but eventually they catch up with us and force us to confront them. The search for meaning and significance sets us apart from animals; we believe it is indicative of having been created in God's image. The day-to-day routine involving work, family, and play is not enough to satisfy these deeper impulses.

For example, Bill Gates is the richest man in the world and has clearly succeeded in many ways, financially, intellectually, and historically. Why did he create a charity that spends millions of dollars in the hope of making people's lives better? We believe it's because a conscious effort to be a positive influence is part of the bigger picture of our lives. It's what helps us make a difference.

We believe that nothing can fully satisfy us apart from a personal relationship with God. But at the same time, He created all human beings, whether they acknowledge it or not, to derive meaning from having some type of impact on the people, events, and circumstances with which they're surrounded throughout life. To live a life that matters: that's influence. To influence in a good way is to live a life that matters. Therefore we invite you to hear and consider any advice that has the ring of truth and practicality.

• • •

Key Points

- Most people have the potential to achieve a greater level of personal influence.
- Influence is a person's ability to shape people and mold outcomes.
- Influence is a combination of clout—something strong, muscular, direct, and intentional—and an intangible, almost mysterious, process.
- The word influence comes from the Latin verb *influere*, meaning to flow in, illustrating what happens in the influence process: one person's life flows into the life and circumstances of another individual.
- We can influence, but we cannot guarantee the outcomes and results.
- Leadership is the part of the iceberg that we see above the surface of the water; influence is the giant mass lurking below and out of sight. Here is how it might be summarized:

  Leadership is visible; influence is out of sight.

  Leadership is usually conscious; influence is often unconscious.

  Leadership is contained; influence crosses boundaries.

  Leadership is immediate; influence is long-term.

  Leadership is public; influence is often behind-the-scenes.

  Leadership is formulaic; influence is mysterious.

  Leadership captivates culture; influence drives culture.

- People generally fall into eight categories regarding their own influence:

  Those who have less clout than they think they do

  Those who have more clout than they think they do

  Those who underapply their clout

  Those who wrongly apply their clout

  Those who have clout in one area but feel powerless in another

Those in the twilight of their career who are reflecting on the transferability and sustainability of their clout

Those in the sunrise of their career who are building their clout

Those who question whether a dirty word like clout can be linked with pure spiritual matters

CHAPTER 2

Wisdom

Life's Greatest Asset

Trust in God, but tie your camel.

—Persian proverb

F *TIME* MAGAZINE HAD BEEN AROUND IN OLD
Testament days (specifically, from 970 to 931 B.C.), Solomon undoubtedly would have earned its Man of the Year distinction—perhaps forty years in a row.

Young Solomon was the son of the great King David of Israel.
When he took over from his father, he was young and untested—
probably only in his early twenties at his inauguration. He went on to
rule for forty years, and during his reign Israel experienced her greatest glory in terms of power, wealth, and status among the other nations of the ancient world.

No one could have imagined a brighter future for young Solomon. But then, he had every advantage. His family legacy and privi-
lege were comparable to those of the English monarchy at the height
of its power, during the reign of Queen Victoria. He inherited all the
wealth his father, David, had accumulated. What else could he possibly need?

Apparently, God decided he needed some help. Appearing to Solomon in a dream, God made a divine offer to grant Solomon whatever he requested. (If this had been an ancient TV game show, the ratings would undoubtedly have shot through the roof as the Israelites sat on the edge of their chairs in the living room, watching and waiting for Solomon's answer: will he choose door number one, door number two, or door number three?)

Look at a passage in 2 Chron. 1:7–12:

> That night God appeared to Solomon and said to him, "Ask for whatever you want me to give you."
>
> Solomon answered God, "You have shown great kindness to David my father and have made me king in his place. Now, Lord God, let your promise to my father David be confirmed, for you have made me king over a people who are as numerous as the dust of the earth. Give me wisdom and knowledge, that I may lead this people, for who is able to govern this great people of yours?"
>
> God said to Solomon, "Since this is your heart's desire and you have not asked for wealth, riches or honor, nor for the death of your enemies, and since you have not asked for a long life but for wisdom and knowledge to govern my people over whom I have made you king, therefore wisdom and knowledge will be given you. And I will also give you wealth, riches and honor, such as no king who was before you ever had and none after you will have."

Solomon could have asked for anything—wealth, respect, the elimination of his enemies, long life—but instead he asked for wisdom and knowledge to rule God's people well. He already had unparalleled status among his peers. He also had wealth and probably knew he would accumulate more. What he didn't have was the wisdom to rule, and in a flash of humility and insight he recognized he didn't have it.

By virtue of his position, Solomon was one of the most influential men alive, but to make that influence stick, to gain true clout as king, he knew he needed wisdom. God, impressed with his choice (if it's possible for God to be impressed), granted Solomon's request and then threw in riches and honor as a bonus.

Elsewhere in Scripture, we see the results of his decision. We learn that Solomon had discernment along with wisdom, and that he was greater than all the kings of the earth in riches and wisdom (I Kings 4:29–34). We see other rulers, such as the Queen of Sheba, testing the extent of his wisdom and honoring God once they see it for themselves (I Kings 10). In the New Testament, Jesus referred to Solomon in all his splendor (Matthew 6). Solomon picked wisdom above riches, honor, and the rest of his options because he saw it as the one virtue that would act as an umbrella for everything else.

My family recently headed for the beaches of Florida for our summer vacation. One day, we found ourselves waiting out a rainstorm in our condo watching classic movies, and *The Absent-Minded Professor* came on; it was the original version of Disney's *Flubber*. Flubber, in case you haven't seen the movie, was a polymer with amazing transformative abilities that came about as the result of a laboratory accident. Anything that touched flubber was changed at the molecular level; its very constitution was altered.

When flubber attached to regular tennis shoes, the person wearing them could spring over the heads of everyone else on the basketball court and perform airborne acrobatics. (Could flubber be the secret of His Airness, Michael Jordan?) It was a good thing the tennis shoes jumped so high because the flubber-coated basketball soared even higher, through the roof. It turned a plain old Chevy into an early smart car that could fly. Flubber was a superagent of transformation.

The same is true of wisdom. Wisdom can radically change the constitution of our lives at the most fundamental level. It enhances and transforms us, allowing us to see, make decisions, and act in a way we couldn't conceive of without it.

What Is Wisdom?

What exactly is this wisdom that Solomon requested? According to other Scripture references to Solomon and the kind of wisdom he possessed, this was not brilliance alone, although Solomon certainly had that in abundance. True wisdom, the kind Solomon was granted, is *the ability to sort out life's options and construct truth so that it makes sense, is useful, and can be passed on to others.*

This kind of wisdom is tied to influence and clout. Wisdom involves seeing from God's perspective. It's being able to climb high in a tree and look far and wide so that we can see to the horizon, with our view unobstructed. Consider a rich and intricate tapestry. If you look at the fabric from the back side, it looks awful. The threads are jumbled and random, the texture is uneven; there's no apparent pattern or beauty. But flip it over and look at it from the correct side, and amazingly the pattern comes into view. This is what wisdom does for us: it lets us see life from the perspective of beauty and pattern.

Again, our definition of wisdom is the ability to sort out life's options and construct truth so that it makes sense, is useful, and can be passed on to others. Wisdom is kind of like horse sense; it's an intuitive ability to discern the correct path. But it's more than horse sense; it's holy horse sense because it involves seeing from God's perspective. A dictionary definition of wisdom is "the ability to choose rightly." That's a good start, but again there's more to it. It's also the ability to detect and sort through options, to navigate through innumerable rocks that can overturn any boat at any turn.

The LINK BETWEEN WISDOM *and* INFLUENCE

Is it possible to be influential without being wise, or to be wise without being influential? We think the two attributes are married; specifically, wisdom enhances and enriches a person's personal influence greatly. Let's look at a few reasons for believing this.

Wisdom purifies my motivation.

Wisdom causes me to perform periodic internal probes to capture and root out selfishness in my motives. Seeking to gain clout and influence with other people in my life carries the risk of becoming consumed with my own interests and hungry for control. Let's face it; we're hard-wired for self-interest, and it takes the divine perspective of wisdom to be brutally honest in our self-examination and motivational inventory. Wisdom acts as an ultrasensitive alarm triggered in our soul whenever we feed our pride. When my action looks as if it is for you but my motivation is really about me, wisdom screams a red alert. It is this wisdom that keeps our conscience clean and our hearts pure.

Wisdom broadens my horizon.

With wisdom, I can see events and decisions from a perspective that would otherwise be impossible. Our friend Ron was an executive at a Fortune 200 company. From all appearances, he had it made, with a successful career, good income, early retirement, and a life of leisure not far down the road. But Ron was restless. One day, he called me and said, "I think I want to be a high school teacher and coach." I picked myself up after falling off my chair. We talked through his decision and the impact it would have on him and his family, and it was obvious that he was doing the right thing. So Ron quit his high-paying corporate job and entered another world. When people found out, they were stunned. Over and over they asked him, "Why? Why would you give up security and money and an influential position to teach . . . *high school?*"

Ron answered that teaching is what he was created to do. It was his calling. He could make a greater contribution of skills and passion in teaching, and for him that was more important than status, money, and the world's definition of success. Sure enough, Ron is now an English honors teacher and coach at a local public high school, and loving it. Without wisdom, it's doubtful that Ron could have gone through with his decision—or even considered it in the first place. But wisdom broadened his horizon. To him, having clout with high school students was more important than being a big shot in the business world. He wanted to channel his influence in a new direction. He climbed the tree and saw the entire farm below, all the way out to the horizon. Wisdom has a way of doing that.

Wisdom clears the complexity.

A term closely related to wisdom is *understanding*. Let's look at this word briefly. Together, the two root words *under* and *stand* convey the idea of seeing clearly thanks to angle and position. If you stand under a tree, you can see birds and squirrels, dead branches, twists in the trunk, patches of sky through the leaves—you "under stand" the tree. Wisdom and understanding enable us to see through to the other side of a complex situation, between and through circumstances, sorting through all the stuff that gets in the way and confuses the picture.

Imagine you're on a path and you encounter a huge sphere blocking the way. The sphere represents a complex issue in life. It looks overwhelming, and the curve of its walls obscures what's on the other side. Your usual response might be to retreat. Or you could bounce off the surface and create an alternative path, rather than tackle what's in front of you. With wisdom, when you approach that life sphere you can see to the other side, sort through the complexities, and weigh your options. Wisdom gives you a whole different perspective, a clear outlook. The more clout and influence you have, the more you will face complex and confusing situations, and the more important wisdom and clarity become.

Wisdom anchors my victories and defeats.

As influential people, we experience both stunning success and devastating failure. Remember that influence can shape, but it cannot guarantee. Circumstances and people turn out both better and worse than we thought. Wisdom—seeing life from God's perspective—helps us take both the peaks and valleys in stride, not giving ourselves too much credit when things go right or placing undue blame on ourselves when they fall apart. It brings stability and continuity to what can sometimes be a wild ride.

WHERE *and* HOW DO WE GET WISDOM?

Now that we know a little bit about what wisdom is, and why it's important if we're seeking to expand our personal influence, how do we go about attaining it? There are several ways.

By asking for it

Wisdom is a gift, and sometimes all we need to do is ask. James 1:5 says, "If any of you lacks wisdom, he should ask God, who gives generously to all without finding fault, and it will be given to him." Imagine a nine-year-old boy saving his paper route or lawn mowing money for a new baseball glove. When the season rolls around and he counts his money, he comes up two dollars short. So he asks his father for help, and his dad gives him enough to make the purchase. Or think of an executive facing a tough challenge in the workplace, and on her own she's just not able to come up with the solution. So she calls her team together for a meeting, and together they pool their resources and brainstorm until they get the answer.

This verse from James is saying precisely that: if you don't have enough wisdom on your own, ask for it, and our heavenly Father will give it to you without holding back. There is no evidence that God's decision to shower Solomon with wisdom was a one-time limited offer. Nor is there any proof that God is on a short supply of wisdom and has to ration it carefully. If we come up short, if we can't see the pattern, if life isn't making any sense, we can just ask for help.

By fearing the Lord

Proverbs 1:7 says the fear of the Lord is the beginning of wisdom. A genuine and healthy relationship with God produces two simultaneous attitudes: one of security and closeness, and another of anxiety and uncertainty. This is how it should be. Remember the story of Jesus in the boat with his disciples in Mark 4? The storm came up and Jesus calmed it with one statement. The disciples were afraid—not of the weather—but of Jesus. "Who is this? Even the wind and the waves obey him!" they asked in terror.

God isn't our casual buddy. When writing about the more awe-inspiring attributes of God, theologians regularly use the phrase "holy other." God is not just like me. He's all-powerful and jealous and perfect and immortal. He is holy and He is other than a mere (although high-octane) mortal. The disciples saw Christ in this light: One who had command over the sea and storm. At the same time, God is our father and cares for us deeply, and this is part of our relationship with Him as well. But it's this healthy tension in our relationship with Him that helps wisdom grow in us.

By trafficking in truth

Are all character traits of equal value, and do all the elements of virtue weigh the same amount? It is an interesting question to ponder. In the test of life, is punctuality as important in defining character as honesty? Are cleanliness and godliness really twins? The topic of wisdom makes us contemplate the disproportionate value of honesty and truthfulness in a person's character makeup. A life of honesty and truthfulness creates a fertile field for wisdom to take root in. If my life is full of dishonesty, lies, and deception, it's difficult for wisdom to grow. Truth is an alignment point for the area of wisdom.

By putting it into practice

Here, we could say, is where we "operationalize" wisdom. The more we draw on and apply wisdom in our lives, the more it produces itself. It's like a water pump; you have to give it a little water in order for much more water to flow strongly and smoothly. Anyone who activates and uses wisdom daily soon finds it growing around itself.

I saw this happen when I started praying for wisdom at an early age. I'm not sure when I started or why—maybe it was at my mother's urging—but for some reason I did. Out of that experience, I realized that wisdom was universal (like flubber). It could help me in everything that was important in my life. It helped with relationships, tasks, and making decisions. Since then I've learned a lot more about wisdom, but I'm very grateful for that early start. It's never too late to do a good thing, or the right thing. We can begin now to ask God to grant us more wisdom every day and then apply it and watch it grow.

The Two Sides of Influence

Part of wisdom's relationship with influence is its role in allowing us to recognize both the possibilities and the limits of our clout. There are two collaborating yet distinct components of influence: *human intentionality* and *divine mystery.* Human intentionality is the part of our influence that we recognize, evaluate, and seek to enhance or improve. Divine mystery is the part that's out of our control but that we must acknowledge and embrace. Because we believe God orchestrates external circumstances within His sovereign plan for humanity, and because we don't always (or even regularly) understand it, we call it divine mystery. Whether you call it fate, cosmic intervention, or even random chance, we doubt you will deny that certain things beyond our reach come to bear on our plans, either helping them reach fruition or hindering them. This external orchestration is the second side of influence.

To see human intentionality and divine mystery working in concert, and to draw a distinction between them, look at the metaphor of the farmer who plants a seed, hoping it will yield a plant that bears fruit. (We take this analogy from the parable of the sower and the seed, found in Mark 4.) The farmer can till the ground, scatter the seed, fertilize the soil, drive off the birds that want to eat the seed for a snack, and clear away encroaching weeds. But he may not know that below the topsoil is unyielding bedrock, and the roots have nowhere to go. Or that a midsummer hailstorm will smash his crop flat. Or that a record-breaking drought is only a month around the corner. On the other hand, the abiding conditions may be so favorable that all he needed to do was toss the seed onto the ground and let nature take care of the rest.

Let's take a closer look at this passage (Mark 4:26–28): "He [Jesus] also said, 'This is what the kingdom of God is like. A man scatters seed on the ground. Night and day, whether he sleeps or gets up, the seed sprouts and grows, though he does not know how. All by itself the soil produces grain—first the stalk, then the head, then the full kernel in the head. As soon as the grain is ripe, he puts the sickle to it, because the harvest has come.'"

In the phrase, "All by itself the soil produces grain," the Greek phrase translated *all by itself* is the same root word from which we get the English term *automatic*. The seed automatically does what it was intended and created to do. The farmer can help create the right conditions, but he can't reprogram the seed or control the circumstances of its growth. In the same way, we can do certain things to bring about intended outcomes, but we can't force those outcomes to occur. Much of the outcome is attributable to divine mystery.

If I show you three seeds and ask you which one will produce the tallest tree, yield the most shade, or create the best-quality lumber, there is no way you can know. Likewise, if we go to the maternity ward of the local hospital and look into the nursery, and you ask me which baby will turn out to be the smartest or most successful, I shrug my shoulders. We can water the soil for the tree and we can line up appropriate parenting mechanisms for the child, but much of the process is the result of divine mystery. We simply don't know what the results will be.

An example of this mystery at work is the recent success of Bruce Wilkinson's runaway best-seller, *The Prayer of Jabez*, a tiny book about an obscure Old Testament passage that rocked the publishing world. The book spent months atop the *New York Times* best-seller list, but it began as a publishing accident. Wilkinson wrote the text as a chapter in a separate book, but the publisher didn't think it fit in that particular context. So the company created a separate title and tossed it out to the public. The book hit a chord, and readers responded with voracious enthusiasm. It generated a volley of conversation among people of faith and otherwise, including some backlash and controversy. Now, many publishers are working tirelessly to produce something similar and to mimic this small volume's success. Who could have predicted the influence that the book would have? Who can really guarantee a similar success path?

"So," you may ask, "why bother? If so much of influence is out of my hands, why should I spend time thinking about it?" Good question. Although it's true that we can't control or predict divine mystery, we shouldn't dismiss it either. Maintaining awareness that we don't have ultimate control, that no matter what we do everything can change in a heartbeat, gives us a healthy perspective and sense of humility and keeps us from feeding the hunger for power and control. We're not God, and—it's a funny thing—God chooses the most interesting times and occasions to remind us of that fact. To approach influence without acknowledging the mysterious side of this topic creates unreal expectations and unhealthy outcomes.

The bulk of this book is about the other side of influence, the side we can do something about: the human intentionality part of the equation. One way to think about influence is to imagine a river. For it to change natural direction, two things are necessary: time and pressure. Over time, with enough pressure, the river gradually begins to follow another course, carving new banks and creating a new path in the landscape.

Human intentionality is like that. If we exert our own thinking, follow consistent principles, and display enough determination, with time (note that it doesn't happen instantaneously) we can affect people and events. There are so many things we have no say in: who we come into contact and form relationships with, what stories we play a part in, the events that occur, the timing of those events. But much is in our control as well: how we react to people and events, the decisions we make, the words we speak. We constantly acknowledge that divine mystery may lift the intended result out of our hands, but we have a responsibility to do what we can to shape things according to the way we see best. A quotable slant on the two sides of influence is found in the admonition to "pray as if everything depended on God, and work as if everything depended on me."

The Right Kind of Clout

Recently I was standing in line in the grocery store and overheard a set of parents talking to their kids about drugs. The mother explained that there are good drugs, which help heal and alleviate pain, and there are bad drugs, which are destructive. The same could be said about many things in life: we need to distinguish between the good kind and the bad kind. This is especially true of our influence. We must examine the motivation and effects of our impact and make sure we're wielding the right clout. Here are some guidelines.

THE RIGHT KIND OF CLOUT WORKS TODAY
BUT DOESN'T HAUNT ME TOMORROW.

If we're looking for an ethical shortcut or engaging in an action that produces harmful consequences down the road—such as negotiating a deal that is financially and personally profitable but that violates personal values—we're not building the right kind of influence.

THE RIGHT KIND OF CLOUT WORKS FOR ME
BUT DOESN'T DISHONOR YOU.

This point is similar to the preceding one, but here the focus is on people. My choices and behavior shouldn't lift me up by crushing others down.

THE RIGHT KIND OF CLOUT INVOLVES BOTH
SHREWDNESS AND INNOCENCE.

In Matthew 10:16, Jesus tells His followers to be "as shrewd as snakes and as innocent as doves." This is a confusing admonition, and many Christians err on the dove side. One of our friends is a highly skilled dentist who has great client relations, but he lets his employees take advantage of him, and it's hurting him personally and professionally.

In our undertakings through Life@Work, we seek to incorporate the best business practices and biblical concepts according to Scripture—not one to the exclusion of the other, as often happens. Recently, we traveled to Chicago to speak to a gathering of business and ministry leaders and to think through issues that involved both faith and business. We made an interesting observation that day. Throughout our time together, the business leaders spoke with confidence and authority about financial matters, strategic vision, and organizational direction. But when asked to address spiritual issues, they backed off in a hurry and said it wasn't their area of expertise. The ministry leaders did the exact opposite. What we need is both sides: the wisdom of a serpent and the gentleness of a dove.

THE RIGHT KIND OF CLOUT IS HANDS-ON PRACTICAL
AND EASILY TRANSFERABLE.

As we've already discussed, a strong temptation for people expanding their influence is self-interest, and this often involves wanting to keep secrets themselves. But if their motives are correct, they should be looking for a way to mentor others by offering practical means to help them build their influence as well. Again, part of the definition of wisdom we present in this book is truth that can be passed on to others.

THE RIGHT KIND OF CLOUT INVOLVES MY HARD WORK BUT
ALSO ACCOUNTS FOR THE MYSTERIOUS ELEMENTS BEYOND ME.

There are, we have said, two sides of influence: human intentionality and divine mystery. I'm not going to become a more effective influence without consciously, deliberately working at it. But at the same time, I must accept and even welcome the fact that I'm not in control, that there are mysterious elements at work as well. When things turn out differently than I plan or want, relinquishing my grip on the situation produces a realistic perspective and healthy sense of humility.

I recently spent an afternoon with a young man I'm coaching through a tough job transition. I'll call him Jeff. Jeff works in Manhattan and earns a significant income, but as a trade for that mountain of money he spends a lot of time on the commuter train and at the office. All the energy he's put into his job in the last fifteen years, including leading his division through a significant restructuring, has started to take a toll. He has four kids at home, he's tired, and he needs a break—maybe even a new job.

Recently Jeff asked for a month off, and his boss agreed to let him take the time. Jeff is a man of faith, so during that month he fully engaged all the issues surrounding his faith: his sense of calling, balance in life, and economic reward. He really wrestled with every aspect of his professional life and its impact on his personal life and spiritual walk. It was so inspiring to watch him make great choices.

When Jeff returned to work, he decided he would sit down with the boss and have a heart-to-heart conversation. But he was concerned that if he were to reveal what was really going on with him, he might risk his leverage in obtaining an exit package. So he and I talked through his approach. One thing we did was scribble out a set of guiding values that would help him in his approach. Here's what we came up with:

1. Handle yourself in such a manner that you can live with yourself long after this decision is made.

2. When possible, if possible, surprise your employers with a display of supernatural grace.

3. Negotiate with shrewdness the greatest walk-away value of your fifteen-year investment.

4. Stay focused on the target, and don't lose sight of the goal.

In this period of his life, Jeff is making a tremendous, admirable effort to develop and use his personal influence wisely. He is acting in a way that will not haunt him later in life. He is making decisions that work for him but don't dishonor other individuals in his life. He is acting with the shrewdness of a snake but the innocence of a dove. He is working through his decision in a way that is practical and may even be transferable to people he has mentored through the years. He is putting forth a great deal of hard work but accepting the reality that other factors also affect the outcome. Jeff is a great example of someone wielding the right kind of clout.

Let's go back to the Old Testament story of Solomon. Unfortunately, the end of the story isn't as satisfying as the beginning. Solomon lost his grip on the ways of wisdom and fell into a lifestyle that wasn't honoring to God or fulfilling of his deepest desires. He began life with dazzling promise but failed because he quit practicing the core of his belief system. The Old Testament book of Ecclesiastes chronicles Solomon's end-of-life reflections on the decisions he made and their impact on his life.

Solomon was a curious mixture. He was an author and composer, administrator and architect, diplomat, trader, horseman, sportsman, and socialite. He seemed to have it all, but it wasn't enough. Chuck Swindoll says that three things brought Solomon down and eroded his life: extravagance (nothing satisfied him any longer), boredom (nothing stimulated him any longer), and disillusionment (nothing anchored him any longer). Solomon lost the single thing that held his life together; the wisdom he had early was no longer in play. He had lost that universal additive called wisdom. Anyone hoping to build a life of sustained personal influence should learn from Solomon: get wisdom early, and never let it get away from you.

• • •

Key Points

- Wisdom is the ability to sort out life's options and construct truth so that it is useful, makes sense, and can be passed on to others. It is an intuitive ability to discern the correct path.
- Wisdom is an asset that, when added, increases anyone's clout.
- Why is there a close link between influence and wisdom?

  Because wisdom purifies my motivation

  Because it broadens my horizon

  Because it clears the complexity

  Because it anchors my victories and defeats
- Influence results from a combination of human intentionality and divine mystery.

- How do we get wisdom?

  By asking for it

  By fearing the Lord

  By trafficking in truth

  But putting it into practice

- Influence needs sound spiritual tempering to make it healthy and effective in the long run.

- What kind of clout is right?

  Right clout works today but does not haunt me tomorrow.

  It works for me but does not dishonor you.

  It involves both shrewdness and innocence.

  It is hands-on-practical and easily transferable.

  It involves my hard work but also accounts for the mysterious elements beyond me.

CHAPTER 3

Aristotle Speaks on Wall Street

Three Ancient Tools of Influence

A man with a testimony is never at the mercy of a man with an argument.

—Anonymous

THE ANCIENT GREEK PHILOSOPHER ARISTOTLE can be credited as one of the most influential people in history in terms of shaping Western society and thought. He had clout, and it lasted. How did he earn such distinction? By teaching and writing about influence.

The biographical information historians have uncovered about Aristotle is thin, but we do know a few details. He was born in 384 B.C. in a part of Macedonia that juts into the Aegean Sea. When he was seventeen years old, he moved to Athens and enrolled in Plato's Academy, where he remained until Plato's death in 347. While there, he began to teach about rhetoric and persuasion; he tutored Alexander, the son of King Philip of Macedonia who went on to conquer much of Europe, Africa, and Asia as Alexander the Great. After Philip's death in 335, Aristotle established his own school of rhetoric in Athens and remained there until the end of his life. He died in 322.

Since then, Aristotle has had enormous cycles of influence throughout history. His ideas have contributed to the study of philosophy, science, and theology—in fact, there are few disciplines that haven't been shaped by his influence. Even though many of his philosophical explanations about natural phenomena have been disproved, his teachings about rhetoric and influence have lived on to become a fundamental (though often unrecognized) part of how we live and think. We are not certain of Aristotle's connection to the world of faith, but he created some time-tested "best practices" that we can review, study, and perhaps replicate. This uncertainty should not keep us from looking to Aristotle for learning. Sound orthodoxy has always taught that all truth has its source in God, which gives us the freedom to reach wide to sources for help. Truth and life are God's patent and trademark.

A Mandate *for* Influence

During the time when Aristotle lived, Greek culture was made up of city-states; Athens was a major one of about sixty thousand people. Although not large compared to our sprawling metropolises, at the time it was the most prominent city in the world. It was governed by a rudimentary form of democracy, quite different from the system we know today. The bulk of Athenian society was made up of women and slaves, but the relatively small population of free men ran the city. Every free man was expected to take a turn periodically participating in city governance, including the law, courts, senate, and policy making. He might be asked to settle a dispute between a merchant and customer, help decide whether to raise taxes, or engage in debate about going to battle with Sparta.

No free man was exempt from participation in this system, and no one was allowed to remain neutral on a given issue. If anyone tried to shirk his responsibility or set himself apart from a debate, the law required that he be exiled and his property confiscated. The result was almost certain death; no one in that day could survive apart from the city and its resources. Ancient Athens was the only culture in the history of civilization, we could say, in which influence was mandatory. The bottom line was that citizens of Athens had to figure out how to be influential or die. Clout wasn't a luxury; it was a life-and-death necessity.

Because of this mandate, schools of rhetoric developed where Athenians could learn how to exert influence. In the oral culture of ancient Athens, rhetoric and influence were closely related. People were persuasive through spoken argument, not through the written word. In fact, the only people who knew how to read and write were slaves, because they kept the records. Free men engaged in verbal debate; oratory skills were valued above all other intellectual enterprise. The schools of rhetoric taught various techniques that Athenians could use to argue a point convincingly.

It was in this environment that Aristotle developed his ideas about rhetoric. His school was only one of many in the city, but it is his teachings with which we are most familiar. Why did his ideas endure and not those of his contemporaries? We're not exactly sure, but a likely theory is that he recorded them in writing and no one else did. (It's worth noting that in a culture that valued influence so highly but writing so little, the most influential teacher proved to be the one who wrote things down.) Because so little written communication exists from other thinkers of that day, we don't really know if Aristotle's ideas were common throughout society or original with him. What we do know is that the content of Aristotle's system of influence endured and that those ideas eventually formed the bedrock of Western thinking. In almost any situation today where we try to exert influence in a particular situation, we draw upon Aristotle's ideas and techniques, though we don't usually know it at the time.

Before we go any further, we should note that Aristotle used the term *persuasion,* by which he meant the process of closing the gap between two people holding divergent ideas. The true end of persuasion, he said, is not just to change someone's mind, but to change his or her will or behavior—to get that person to do something different, not just think something different. This is essentially the same as our definition of influence, the process of shaping people and outcomes. What Aristotle called persuasion, we call influence.

At SCHOOL *with* ARISTOTLE

An interesting note about Aristotle is that his school of rhetoric was not the most popular in Athens. The prominent school at the time was led by a man named Isocrates, who taught his followers how to persuade through the use of emotion. Then, as now, playing to emotion was a common way to accomplish one's goal. (We see this today in weepy commercials for long-distance phone service and televangelists who thunder and whimper, hoping to provoke an emotional response—usually measured in dollars and cents—from the audience.) Aristotle, in contrast, contended that argument from emotion would not influence anyone for any length of time. Emotionally based decisions are not sustainable, he said; they last only as long as the emotional response, and volatile emotion tends to fade as quickly as it arises. When it does fade, so does the will to act on the decision at its base.

Aristotle taught his followers a rational means of persuasion with arguments based on logic, which were more difficult to construct but created a deeper and longer-lasting impact. In presenting your case, he said, there are two kinds of proof, or argument, you can make: artistic and nonartistic. A nonartistic proof is based on available information and contains "just the facts." An example of a nonartistic proof would be a legal document, a contract, or witness testimony in court. It contains data that are readily available and discernible without any kind of artful construction. But most human interaction revolves around artistic proof: argument in which you have to make your case. If you don't make your case, your argument and the reasons behind it are not obvious and not likely to persuade anyone to your way of thinking.

Creation of artistic proof, Aristotle said, is the province of rhetoric or reason. He described rhetoric as the faculty of observing, in a given case, the available means of persuasion and identifying the best one for presenting your argument. This definition implies that there is no one-size-fits-all argument that can be adapted to any situation. Becoming skillful in rhetoric involves being able to observe a situation and an audience and choosing from your rhetorical toolbox the device that is most likely to be effective and persuasive in that situation.

One such tool might be a story that illustrates your point in a way that is clear to your audience. For example, the famous fabler Aesop, Aristotle tells us, used a story to defend an individual in the Greek city of Samos who was on trial for his life. His crime? He was much wealthier than the average citizen, and the public believed that the only way he could have become so rich was by taking money away from them. So Aesop created a fable. A fox was crossing a river and got stuck in a hole in the rocks. Unable to free herself, she was attacked by fleas, and the itching was miserable. A hedgehog happened to come roaming by and saw the fox's plight. He offered to swish away the fleas, but the fox declined, saying, "By now, the fleas have drunk their fill of my blood and are not bothering me as much. But if you drive them away, hungry fleas will take their place and completely finish me off."

Aesop's point was that the man he was defending would take nothing from the citizens of Samos because he was wealthy already. But if they put him to death, other people would look to become rich in his place and empty the citizens' pockets completely. Sometimes an illustration, whether a true story or a made-up one, can drive a point home in a way nothing else can.

The LINES *of* ARGUMENT

In his teachings, Aristotle identified twenty-eight lines of argument, or ways to influence someone's thinking. We use them today in our everyday interactions, in our work, and in civic life—again, whether we know they came from Aristotle or not. Becoming familiar with these lines of logical argument can help us become influential in our own lives. Some of the distinctions among the twenty-eight lines are rather fine, so for purposes of clarity and conciseness we've distilled them down to fourteen.

1. CONSEQUENCES

Any advocated action inevitably results in both good and bad consequences. This line of argument uses the consequences as a reason to urge that a thing should or should not be done. For example, in debating whether to go to war against Iraq, many legislators were opposed because of the potential loss of human life. They believed the consequence (death of U.S. soldiers) was not worth the action (war). Here's another illustration of an argument from consequences: "If we fire Bill without telling people why he was let go, everyone in his unit may think they're in jeopardy of losing their job." Kids are notoriously and innately skilled at this line of argument—especially when they want to get out of work.

2. Opposites

This strategy involves asking what will occur if a proposed action is undertaken and what will happen if it's not. For example, a company has proposed to buy office space instead of renting it, because renting gives no return on investment and buying gives a significant return. Or a taxpayer is trying to decide whether to hire an accountant to do her taxes. If she does, she'll have to pay $1,000, which is a little beyond her budget. But if she doesn't hire an accountant and doesn't receive all her deductions, she could lose significantly more money. Arguing from opposites is a common strategy in the consulting world ("If you hire me, it will cost you this much, but if you don't, it will cost you more"). Coaches also use this argument: "Stay in shape this summer or you won't start in the fall and you'll have to run extra after practice."

3. Time frames

This type of argument uses time as a factor in deciding whether to take action or not. For example, planning a trip near the end of October instead of the end of November avoids Thanksgiving delays. Or if a company waits to launch a product, a competitor may beat the company with its own product. Any area of life or work involving deadlines is connected to time, which can be used in persuasion as a logical form of influence.

4. Motive

This line of argument considers the underlying reason for some-one undertaking or avoiding a certain action. Sound familiar? The legal system relies heavily on this line of argument. The jury considers a suspect's motive to help decide guilt or innocence; once a suspect is found guilty, a judge weighs motive in determining a heavy or light sentence. Someone shopping for a new car also uses argument from motive when she concludes that the sales person at the dealership wants to sell her a more expensive car because he'll receive a bigger commission. Considering the motive can often persuade someone for or against a certain action.

5. Precedent

This method uses data from a previous decision or action to justify or argue for or against proposed action. The strategy asks, What has happened in the past that gives us an idea of what might happen in the future? Does this proposal line up with our actions and decisions in the past? Again, our courts use this type of logic extensively; previous court decisions guide a current case being argued. Or if someone decides to book a room at the Marriott because another hotel has messed up his reservation on the last three trips, he is using an argument from precedent. Any business that relies on repeat-customer allegiance relies heavily on this argument.

6. INCONSISTENCY

Inconsistency involves evaluating an argument or action by noting any contradiction in date, word, evidence, or act. Here's an example of someone using argument from inconsistency: "First she said one thing, now she says something completely different. She can't have it both ways. We need to reject her proposal." A buyer sitting across from a salesperson is listening for inconsistency. Most parents listen for it when a child rolls out requests for the weekend. Anyone looking for a reason to dismiss someone or say no to a request is often able to do so on the basis of inconsistency.

7. DEFINING TERMS

Words and terms have latitude of meaning. This line of argument allows you to use the same term as someone on the opposite side of the issue but define it to your advantage: "I agree that we must move quickly on this issue, but do you define 'quickly' as 'without planning'?" Or "It's true that we need to empower people, but empowerment does not mean allowing them to work without accountability."

8. MODIFYING KEY WORDS

The strategy of modifying key words uses change in phrasing to make a point and redirect attention toward your argument. Rush Limbaugh used this tactic during President Bill Clinton's first bid for the presidency: He referred to Arkansas as "Arksylvania" (alluding to Transylvania, not Pennsylvania), to Bill Clinton as "Count Taxula," and to the vice-presidential candidate as "Algore" (as in Igor). By modifying three key words, he drew a sinister picture. This case illustrates a kind of argument often shrouded in humor, but it's extremely effective. Many politicians are skilled in this line of persuasion.

9. Dividing topics

Another kind of argument divides an issue into its constituent parts and deals with each segment separately. An executive is dividing topics when he explains that the company needs to be restructured along "total quality management principles." Specifically, he says, the process involves two elements: driving out fear and eliminating barriers between staff areas. Although "restructuring" sounds complicated, the executive distills it down to two key elements to gain support and accomplish the task.

10. False impressions

The false-impression line of argument seeks to explain that things aren't always as they seem. A speaker who appears nervous and unsure of herself during a presentation might give the impression that she has something to hide or is ill-prepared. But if an audience member remarks that this is her first time speaking in front of a large group, this changes the impression and might convince people to think differently. This is a false-impression argument.

11. Changing minds

People often change their mind over time. Even if someone took a particular position previously, it might be different now. Here is a case of someone using changing minds in his argument: "It's true that our CEO used to take a dim view of employee teams, calling them 'the fad of the moment' in a speech three years ago. But our teams have since proven themselves crucial to the business plan, and we've received no indication he still feels the same way."

12. Speaking publicly and privately

There is often a discrepancy between what people approve of publicly and what they endorse privately, and this discrepancy can be used to make a case. For example: "You need a private facilitator to come here and conduct your focus groups. Unless you get someone from outside the company, the people in the group might not be very open."

13. Greater to lesser

If a pair of events are under discussion and the more difficult of the two has already been accomplished, then the less difficult and more believable event seems possible. A mother might use this kind of argument on her son: "Jeremy, since you got a first-place ribbon on your science fair project, surely you can figure out how to get your room cleaned up by dinnertime."

14. CAUSE AND EFFECT

Cause and effect allows you to argue forward from the cause to the effect, or backward from the effect to the cause: "We would like to congratulate this team on achieving exceptional results during the last quarter. Their hard work made it possible." Or: "On the basis of our experience with other retailers your size and category, we think that if the following plan is put into effect, it will yield significant growth in market share." An entrepreneur uses this line of argument in presenting a forecast and proposal for future direction.

Do any of these lines of argument sound familiar? Have you used any of these methods with success? Did you know you were drawing on ancient Greek rhetorical wisdom? The fourteen lines of argument are so grafted into our society and way of thinking that we use them and don't even realize it. Being aware of all available arguments, not just two or three, can help us be more influential.

GADGETS *and* GIZMOS

The other night, I couldn't sleep, so I read for a while and then watched some late-night (actually early-morning) television. I flipped through black-and-white sports reruns, and I perused sales pitch after sales pitch. The sellers fell into two groups: those peddling God and religion and those selling everything else. I don't have the stomach for the TV God-sellers, so I went to the other group. One program featured a gentleman selling home gadgets. All these gizmos were touted to make my home run better and the work easier. There were grippers to open jars, supercleaning agents that made dirt flee in terror, pole-extension instruments to clean cobwebs and windows, and so on. Fortunately, I made it through the infomercial without going for my credit card, but I was astonished at all that had been invented to make my home life easier.

This is how it is with Aristotle's fourteen lines of argument—strategies that can be applied in the area of intentional influence. If you're trying to persuade someone from one way of thinking to another, you need the right equipment, and the fourteen lines of argument are handy, easy-to-use tools in your influence toolbox.

About a year ago, my older daughter decided she wanted a mobile phone. According to her, everyone at school, at church, in the neighborhood, and around the entire world that was her age or even close to her age had a cell phone. She'd asked for one for Christmas and on other occasions, but she had yet to see it, much to her frustration. The problem was her father.

We were at a congressional-level gridlock in the cell phone debate. My daughter declared that a cell phone was a gift, and she wanted to see it wrapped up in pretty paper and presented as a surprise. The $21 monthly fee was an inconsequential part of the package. I saw a mobile phone as an ongoing responsibility that would be more or less expensive depending on the discipline and self-control of the user. I held out that cell phones and cars were in a different category from CD players and new clothes. Both of us being stubborn, we held to our positions.

Two weeks before her birthday, we had a meltdown. Beside herself and near tears, she said all she wanted for her birthday was a cell phone, and she argued and pleaded and threatened. She thought she would wear me down, but she was misguided by equating my weak knees with a weak will. "Why?" she asked. "Why won't you let me have a phone?" I listened but didn't answer.

Later that evening, we were in the car by ourselves. I reclarified my thinking to her. "I have never said you couldn't have a cell phone, but I see the issue differently than you do. I have said I would not purchase a cell phone as a gift with no strings on your side. You can stay on your side of the fence, or you can come over to my side and persuade me to see it differently."

I explained the world of influence and gave her some Aristotelian fatherly tips. I told her she needed to find something we could agree upon, such as how to pay for the phone, and go from there. I told her to ask me some questions, find out what I was thinking, and answer my objections. Once she did that, she needed to present me with a win-win solution.

The point was not that I didn't want my daughter to have a cell phone. I wanted her to learn from and use this situation as an early test run for a more mature approach to the world of managing money. I knew that right around the corner was buying a car, and this was a dress rehearsal. I wanted her to feel the responsibility of monthly payments and to realize how big the gap can be between budgeting and behavior.

Well, she did it. She picked up a few of Aristotle's lines of argument and influenced me toward her desired outcome. Within days she had the telecommunication world by the tail with her pink-covered cell phone. Her rhetorical toolbox is a lot fuller than it was, and I'm ready to accede to her next time if she persuades me.

The ARISTOTELIAN TRIANGLE

Being influential doesn't stop with identifying and using the appropriate line of argument. According to Aristotle, every situation involves a system of interacting elements that work together to establish whether someone is influential and how someone is influenced. The core of Aristotle's system of influence is what we now call the Aristotelian Triangle. It has three elements—logos, pathos, and ethos—that determine a person's persuasiveness. Without any one element, the argument of the influencer falls flat.

Logos

The first leg of the triangle is *logos,* a Greek term that is rich and layered in meaning but in essence can be interpreted as *word.* In this context, logos refers to the content of a person's message and the structure

Aristotle's Triangle

Ethos

Logos   Pathos

of his or her argument. For a university professor, it's the lectures she prepares and the readings she assigns her students. A trial lawyer's logos is his opening and closing arguments and how he presents his evidence. For a sales representative, logos is the list of reasons a client would benefit from purchasing a certain product. Without a meaningful and well-developed message, all the snazzy embellishments of presentation won't do any good. If someone wants to exert influence in a particular area, she must identify the best words with which to communicate and present them in the best way possible.

Pathos

The second element of a person's influence is *pathos,* a unique leg of the triangle in that it depends not on the influencer but on the audience. In Aristotle's day, pathos was the response of the audience while the act of speaking was occurring. Today it can refer specifically to a speaker-audience situation, but in a broader sense it can mean the general environment within which an argument is being made: physical location, social milieu, or political context. Surrounding circumstances and their effect on an audience, as well as the audience's reaction while the effort to influence is taking place, all affect the outcome of the process. An executive is leveraging pathos when he takes a client out to the golf course to do business. The client, it is hoped, will be much more favorably disposed to the message out on the links on a sunny afternoon than if he were sitting in a stuffy, windowless conference room.

Ethos

The third leg of the triangle, *ethos,* refers to a person's credibility; it's the same Greek root that gives us the word *ethics.* Ethos pertains to the character of the speaker and how the audience perceives that character. It involves two stages: antecedent ethos and immediate ethos. Antecedent ethos is the listeners' perception of the speaker before she even opens her mouth—it comes before the act of speaking. When the president gets up to deliver the State of the Union address, U.S. citizens have an opinion of him as a person before he says a word. The same goes for the CEO of a publicly traded company at a shareholder meeting. If the company's stock has recently fallen, it's a pretty sure thing that the stockholders are going to have an idea of what they think of the person at the helm before he gives his speech. The other part of ethos, immediate ethos, takes place during the presentation. A speaker fails to live up to listeners' expectations, or meets them, or exceeds them. Their resulting judgment of the speaker's character helps determine whether he or she ends up influencing them significantly.

The KEY LINK

Although all three elements of the Aristotelian Triangle—logos, ethos, and pathos—are fundamental to the influence process, Aristotle believed that the most important element was ethos. It's the credibility of the speaker that has the most potential to make or break the effectiveness of his message. It also is the most difficult element to deliberately construct or reconstruct after it has been shattered, especially since creation or recovery of credibility proceeds case by case. Who I am is who I am. I cannot change my character in time for my speaking engagement at 2:00 P.M. Thursday, and I can't fool my listeners into thinking I'm someone I'm not. An audience has an uncanny ability to detect phoniness, and in general, people hate phonies. If I'm caught posing as someone or something contrary to my true nature, my ability to influence virtually disappears.

ARISTOTLE *at the* FRONT DOOR

So, what does all this mean for us today? If I'm attempting to become more influential, to create a positive impact within my spheres of existence and my relationships, what does the Aristotelian Triangle really do for me? It tells me three things: If I want to be influential in my life, I must have *a message that's meaningful (logos), an audience that's receptive (pathos), and a life that's believable (ethos).*

First of all, my message must have meaning and worth in and of itself. If it's like an attractive storefront with empty shelves behind it, there's no value to anyone. In the commercial world, you can't prop up a product or service that's overvalued forever. If Volvo says it makes the safest car, that message must be true. If a large number of people are suddenly being injured or killed in accidents involving Volvos, car buyers who are conscientious about safety will go elsewhere.

Second, it's important to have an audience that's receptive. Let's go back to our Karl Marx example from Chapter One. He died in poverty and obscurity, and his message seemed destined to languish. But when the Industrial Revolution caused chaotic social upheaval and people began to chafe against the resulting suffering and poverty, the situation was ripe for his message to explode in influence. Much of the responsiveness of our audience and environment is beyond our control and in the purview of divine mystery, but there are small things we can do to enhance our ability to influence, such as watch our timing.

Third, I must have a life that's believable. We stand behind Aristotle's claim that having integrity and credibility is the most important aspect of a person's ability to influence. The root word of *integrity* (from which we also get *integer* and *integral*) means being consistent from beginning to end, front to back, the same inside as outside. When we deliver a message, whether to a son or daughter, a friend, a board of trustees, or an arena filled with thousands of people, our listeners will ask, "Are you real? Are you who you say you are or seem to be? Are you the same in private as you are in public?" The answer they get is instrumental in their decision to act on our message.

As we write this, there's a heated senatorial election in going on in our state. The other day, I was flipping through TV channels, and I saw back-to-back ads for the two leading candidates. I counted at least half a dozen lines of argument each candidate used to try to sway my vote and leverage his clout. I watched as each candidate worked the pathos angle by being shown in favorable settings—(full color, casual clothing, surrounded by family, in church, with flags, with the elderly, in the state office, and even in hunting clothing). Then they showed the opposing candidate, trying to undermine his pathos and ethos (homely, pitiful, black-and-white snapshots that looked like a criminal lineup after a jailbreak). The politicians were using Aristotelian principles right and left in their attempt to influence me.

As illustrated by these election ads, although the concepts of influence are almost two and a half millennia old, they're as relevant today as they were in ancient Athens. The next few chapters explore these ideas and their application in greater depth.

• • •

KEY POINTS

- Rhetoric is the faculty of observing, in a given case, the available means of persuasion.

- Aristotle's fourteen lines of argument can help anyone upgrade his or her personal influence:

  Consequences

  Opposites

  Time frames

  Motive

  Precedent

  Inconsistency

  Defining terms

  Modifying key words

  Dividing topics

  False impressions

  Changing minds

  Speaking publicly and privately

  Greater to lesser

  Cause and effect

- The three components of Aristotle's ancient triangle have incredible relevance for today's culture:

  Logos The content of a person's speech, the mind of the speaker, the structure of the speaker's argument

  Pathos The response of the audience during the speaker's presentation

  Ethos A person's credibility; antecedent ethos refers to a person's credibility before she begins her speech and is based on the audience's prior knowledge of the speaker, while immediate ethos refers to the credibility of the speaker during the speaking event itself

- If I want to be influential, I must have a message that is meaningful (logos), an audience that is receptive (pathos), and a life that is believable (ethos).

4

Logos

A Message That Is Meaningful

Flattery is counterfeit money which,
but for vanity, would have no circulation.

—La Rochefoucauld

T HE FIRST FOOTBALL GAME WAS RIGHT AROUND
the corner, in less than ten days. The evening air had a tinge of fall
crispness, and the bleachers were overflowing with parents, alumni, students, and other high school sports enthusiasts. The team had just completed its annual Red-White game for the fans to watch so they could
pledge cash to the booster club, purchase as much team paraphernalia
as they need to prove their support, and listen to the coaches.

It happens every year in junior high, high school, college, and even
the pros. In late summer and early fall, all over America, whether it's a
handful of pickups gathered in West Texas, thousands of fans at Notre
Dame, or millions of remote-ready TV viewers watching an NFL pre-
view, the scene is essentially the same. The head coach gathers the team
and sometimes the fans, and he lays out an argument of where the season is headed. He tries to ignite enthusiasm and hope but leave enough
wiggle room to allow the possibility of less-than-hoped-for performance.

He weaves the words and hurls the anecdotes to encourage players, fans, and the other coaches working with his team to get on board for a successful season.

Down the street, the annual meeting of the locally based Fortune 100 company is going on. It has an amazingly similar feel. Whether a company is public or private, small or large, regional or national, most hold an annual meeting. This is a time for senior leaders to update everyone on the past year's successes and outline the journey ahead. The leader lays out the vision for the next twelve to twenty-four months, which he hopes will come across as logical, emotional, and influential.

The CEO and the head football coach have something in common: they both hope to exercise their clout to persuade members of their audience—even themselves—that a successful season or year lies ahead. During this preseason pep talk, they are engaging the logos process in full stride.

Daily Delivery

We live in an era in which information is a key commodity. Not since the invention of the printing press has the world seen such an explosion in the influence and reach—the sheer power—of information. Mergers between entities such as AOL and Time Warner have created massive deliverers of "content," the catch-all term that encompasses everything from diaper advertisements to analysis of tension in the Middle East. They deliver information on best practices in cooking, financial analysis and trends, sports entertainment for anything remotely close to being called sport, golden oldies, full-length movies, self-help gurus, and the pet psychic (we can't forget channel surfing and running across that one—I must tell you that a number of dogs have been joining our chocolate Labrador in our back yard at certain coordinated times; I think maybe they're hooked on the pet psychic and are watching the show through my bedroom window). Along with this information explosion has come a communication explosion. Cell phones and e-mail have joined more traditional methods of connectivity, resulting in our being in touch with anybody at any time and having access to content from just about anywhere.

In this information age, we all give out and receive thousands of messages daily. We might not have a million-dollar budget to aid our annual meeting or the excitement of a Friday night football game, but we live in a world of messages. In fact, it's becoming more and more difficult to escape that world.

Mission Impossible: 2, the Tom Cruise blockbuster of a few years ago, opens with an ironic image on this state of affairs. Ethan Hunt, Cruise's character, is on holiday, climbing cliffs thousands of feet above the ground. Because he has not informed anyone of his location, he has temporarily eluded his higher-ups. Nevertheless, they track him down by helicopter and deliver his assignment, beginning with the familiar words, "This is your mission, should you choose to accept it." The underlying point, which rings true to a contemporary audience despite its fictional setting, is that no location, no matter how remote or forbidden, is beyond the reach of today's information and communications technology.

We are bombarded by messages from many directions and many sources. In this constant flow of messaging, it has become more and more important that we sort out the meaningful messages from the spam. Also, in considering our own personal influence and clout, we must rigorously examine the messages we send to determine whether they have the substance and relevance to cut through the noise of competing information in the lives of those we hope to affect.

WORDS, MIND, *and* PERSON

Creating and delivering a meaningful message is what logos is all about. Let's look more closely at what the word meant to Aristotle. In the context of persuasive speaking, which is the main emphasis of Aristotelian rhetoric, logos refers to the actual, literal words spoken; it is the speech itself. But it also refers to the mind of the speaker during the speech, the structure of the argument, and the underlying reasoning used to make a point (we get the word *logic* from *logos*).

A startlingly clear example of this idea is the opening verse of the Gospel of John, which refers to Jesus Christ as *logos,* translated here as *the Word*: "In the beginning was the Word, and the Word was with

God, and the Word was God. He was with God in the beginning" (John 1:1).

John continues to use the word *logos* for Jesus throughout the chapter. By choosing this terminology, John is describing Jesus' message, His mind, and His person, all wrapped up in one idea. A commentary note in the NIV Study Bible puts it this way: "Greeks used this term not only of the spoken word but also of the unspoken word, the word still in the mind—the reason. When they applied it to the universe, they meant the rational principle that governs all things."

The concept of logos revolves around words, the mental process, and reason. When Aristotle talked about lines of argument, the use of example, or an effective syllogism, he was talking about logos. Effective persuasion, he said, was identifying and using the best argument in a given situation. There's no logos template that can be stamped out and used every time; by definition, logos involves the active mental process of sifting through options and constructing one's thoughts in a way likely to be convincing.

The purpose of this idea in ancient Greece was mostly to help a person stand before a political assembly and argue a point effectively, but it has a broader application for us today. A message is not only a speaker giving a speech; it goes beyond to a lobbyist pontificating over a meal in Washington, D.C. Logos involves anybody who touts a product, a service, or a lifestyle as better than others. If a car dealer says, "Buy this car from me and here's what I'll do for you," that's a clear message. It's the dealer's thoughts couched in words delivered in a certain way.

A vendor who opens her treasure chest of products with the argument that they belong on the shelves of a certain retailer—that's logos. A coach delivers a message (logos) when he breaks down a game play by play, to show where the team's weaknesses lie and what the players need to work on. E-mail is a message. So are a voice mail, a presentation, an advertisement, and a casual chat. Products and services can even be considered a message because they say something about the company that produced them. They all involve principles of logos. An understanding of logos helps determine whether those messages are meaningful or not. Let's look at some ways of constructing a meaningful message.

Finding *a* Common Place

In Chapter Two, we looked at Aristotle's lines of argument. Here's a quick review:

- Consequences: weighing the results of possible actions
- Opposites: looking at both sides of an issue
- Time: considering how time affects a potential course of action
- Motive: evaluating a person's intentions
- Precedent: using a previous decision or action to guide a current one
- Defining terms: using definition to your advantage
- Modifying key words: putting a twist on important words or phrases
- Dividing topics: breaking an issue down into its basic elements
- False impressions: considering how something may be different from what it seems
- Changing minds: acknowledging that people can come to think differently over time
- Speaking publicly and privately: leveraging the possibility that someone may speak or act differently behind closed doors
- Greater to lesser: using accomplishment of a more complex and difficult challenge to support a current enterprise
- Cause and effect: arguing forward from the cause to the effect, or backward from the effect to the cause

The idea, you will remember, is to be familiar with all the possibilities and use the most effective tool for a particular situation. There's a problem pilots sometimes experience when flying an aircraft. Even though they're trained to constantly scan all the gauges, they sometimes favor one or two and neglect the rest—a situation known as instrument lock. For instance, a plane can have great altitude and plenty of fuel, but if its air speed is too low and the pilot doesn't correct, she'll go into a tailspin. It can also happen with these lines of argument; we tend to favor certain ones over others, which can diminish our effectiveness and our clout. If I use only precedent and cause and effect and those methods don't resonate with my audience, or if another messenger uses a more effective line of argument, I fall short in my ability to be influential.

Another powerful concept tied to logos that was first articulated by Aristotle is the idea of the common place. When I am trying to influence someone, and there's a gap in thought, belief, or action between the other person and me, I need a bridge. The process of influence involves closing that chasm, or creating a bridge over it. An essential step at the beginning of the process is to set up a common place, a thought or issue that we can agree on. Once we've established the common place, we can use the lines of argument to persuade someone to proceed down a new path. It is much easier to do this from a common place than from opposite sides of the canyon.

Lack of a common place is in part why the abortion debate is so contentious in our country. There is no agreement on when life begins—at conception, birth, or somewhere in between. So the debate continues to rage, with little hope of resolution.

I experienced this process not long ago when I was in the car listening to National Public Radio. A news analyst came on with a commentary asserting that Washington, D.C., ought to have home rule. The city doesn't have its own senator or representative but answers directly to Congress. I said to myself, *Who cares? I don't live in Washington, D.C. This doesn't pertain to me.* But before I could switch the station, the commentator continued with the statement that the only U.S. citizens who have taxation without representation are convicted felons and residents of the District of Columbia.

Then he had my attention. Taxation without representation is why a bunch of colonial vigilantes dressed up as Indians and dumped tea into the Boston Harbor. It's why we fought the Revolution. It's not fair; it's not right—legal citizens should have adequate representation in the federal government if they help fund that government. This analyst had found a common place, and he proceeded to walk step by logical step toward his conclusion. I listened to every word of his commentary and found myself agreeing with him by the end.

Jesus used the common place constantly when He spoke to His disciples and the crowds that followed Him throughout His ministry. He spoke of bread and water, laborers in the field, masters and servants—all touchstones of cultural life that hearers would identify with and respond to. From those common places, He proceeded to unveil dramatic truths about the kingdom of God that would have been impossible to absorb otherwise. We too should look for the common place as we seek to influence. The common place is the staging ground for the pilgrimage to a new reality we would like the other person to embark upon.

Spoken Versus Written

Part of the effectiveness of our logos message relates to the method we use to convey it. We generally need to put as much thought into the choice of vehicle for our message as we do into the message itself. Written communication is the best strategy in many cases. Writing allows us to think clearly through an issue from beginning to end, to lay out our points logically and carefully, to draft and revise as many times as necessary. Some topics are difficult or potentially explosive to talk about in person; writing can avoid spontaneous combustion in a face-to-face conversation. Writing conveys a sense of weight and gravity, telling the other person that this subject is important enough to you that you took the time to put it down on paper. This is why a spouse sometimes writes a letter to another spouse, parents write a letter to their child, or an employer composes a memo to an employee.

But writing carries risk as well. Written words have a long shelf life; they sit around in an e-mail in-box or on a desk or coffee table to be read and reread—maybe more times than you would think possible. Written words are divorced from tone of voice, expression, and gesture, which may cause them to come across differently (usually more strongly) than you intended. This is especially a risk with e-mail; have you ever typed a quick off-the-cuff remark that caused misunderstanding and resentment because the receiver couldn't see your smile and misinterpreted your meaning?

We have two friends who are avid writers and debaters. They realized they had an issue of conflict in a certain area, and they started e-mailing each other about it. Suddenly you would have thought they were arguing a Supreme Court case. The matter was fairly inconsequential, but they poured enormous energy into writing, editing, responding, and arguing their points, and this molehill exploded into an enormous mountain. E-mail has its advantages, but we need to use it with caution. We don't always have a choice, but when we do, we should consider whether the message is better given as a spoken word or a written word.

It's often the smartest move to save our communication for face-to-face discussion. Some issues don't belong in writing, or even on the phone: conflict, emotion, finances, anything that has the possibility for misinterpretation that needs to be clarified through dialogue. If there are two sides of a situation and we must reach an agreement, the conversation probably has to take place in person. I remember a situation where one of my friends called and wanted to talk. He was on the road and wanted to make me aware of his interest in talking through a situation. But he didn't want to talk it over on the phone. So we agreed to a face-to-face meeting and put it on the calendar. Waiting until we were person-to-person worked out much better.

Taming *the* Tongue

A message is constructed around words and phrases. We use thousands of words every day. But are they good words? Are they right and persuasive? A single word is powerful. Tied together, words are as strong a tool of influence as there is.

Gaining control of our words is a full-time, lifelong assignment. We commence building our communication style as soon as we begin to speak, and along the way we pick up patterns from our family, the workplace, significant influences in our lives, and the media. Some of our communication is good, and some is not so good. The problem with language is that not all words are created equal. One slip-up with the tongue isn't equal to one good usage. I can't tell my wife she looks ugly and then turn around and tell her she looks great and expect those words to have the same impact. Negative messages carry different weight.

The small, practical book of James in the New Testament offers day-to-day advice on all kinds of topics, including some strong words on our speech and the challenge of taming the tongue:

When we put bits into the mouths of horses to make them obey us, we can turn the whole animal. Or take ships as an example. Although they are so large and are driven by strong winds, they are steered by a very small rudder wherever the pilot wants to go. Likewise the tongue is a small part of the body, but it makes great boasts. Consider how a great forest is set on fire by a small spark. The tongue also is a fire, a world of evil among the parts of the body. It corrupts the whole person, sets the whole course of his life on fire, and is itself set on fire by hell.

All kinds of animals, birds, reptiles and creatures of the sea are being tamed and have been tamed by man, but no man can tame the tongue. It is a restless evil, full of deadly poison.

With the tongue we praise our Lord and Father, and with it we curse men, who have been made in God's likeness [James 3:3–9].

In this comprehensive, graphic analysis of our speech, we can gain insight into speaking and using words correctly.

The tongue has disproportionate influence (3:3–5). Think about the size of the tongue. Proportionally, this two-ounce slab of muscle between our teeth is more powerful than any other muscle in our body. It carries tremendous power for good or evil as well. To drive home this point, James uses three vignettes from life.

"The bit and the horse"— suggests how the tongue controls great power. A small bit in a horse's mouth can control the animal's actions. Think of a giant Belgian draft horse. With its size and power, it could do anything it wants. But a tiny bit balanced between its teeth tells it when to start, where to go, when to stop. The tongue has disproportionate influence in that it can wield great power.

"The rudder and the ship"—says the tongue sets definite direction. Whether you're talking about a small sailboat or a giant cruise ship, both operate on the same model, directed and guided by the small device of the rudder. This is how the tongue operates in disproportionate influence.

"The forest and the spark"—tells us the tongue causes great destruction. One spark can result in great desolation. Once a woman in

Colorado started a small fire and sparks flew to nearby trees, hundreds of thousands of acres were devastated by the flames. The tongue carries the same kind of massive influence. The power of words is something we should take into consideration with soberness and care. One wrong word can set off a forest fire of destruction.

The tongue is inherently unruly and needs training (3:7–9). My son went to a friend's house one weekend, and the friends happened to be raising a bear cub. It turns out that mother bears give birth during the winter when they're hibernating; sometimes when they're floating in and out of their winter sleep, they're not at the top of their mama bear game. One female bear had five or six cubs over the winter. A state park ranger who is a friend of the family of my son's friend said he'd been watching the bear in her den and that she had too many cubs to take care of. He needed to find someone to raise the cub for a time, and then the state would send it to a zoo. So the family of my son's friend took the cub for six months, and during this time my son visited.

The cub was scheduled to be taken to the zoo the very next week. As you can imagine, my son had a wonderful time playing with the cub. But as he was leaving, the cub tackled him. It was playing, but the force knocked my son over. He was glad the bear was still smaller than he was. Bears are designed to be wild—it's inherent in their DNA. We can try to tame or train them, but they're built wild and they generally stay wild.

The tongue is also inherently unruly and needs much training. The role of a single word is powerful; without constant effort, it can wreak incomparable destruction.

The book of Proverbs has a lot to say about the right kind of words and the wrong kind. Here are words of the sort we should strive to cultivate in our conversation and in building our influence and the good kind of clout.

- *Wise counsel and sound advice.* "A man finds joy in giving an apt reply—and how good is a timely word!" (Prov. 15:23). "Perfume and incense bring joy to the heart, and the pleasantness of one's friend springs from his earnest counsel" (Prov. 27:9).
- *Honest feedback and caution.* "A rebuke impresses a man of discernment more than a hundred lashes a fool" (Prov. 17:10). "Wounds from a friend can be trusted, but an enemy multiplies

kisses" (Prov. 27:6). "A word aptly spoken is like apples of gold in settings of silver. Like an earring of gold or an ornament of fine gold is a wise man's rebuke to a listening ear" (Prov. 25:11–12).

• *Encouragement and kindness.* "Reckless words pierce like a sword, but the tongue of the wise brings healing" (Prov. 12:18). "An anxious heart weighs a man down, but a kind word cheers him up" (Prov. 12:25). "The tongue that brings healing is a tree of life, but a deceitful tongue crushes the spirit" (Prov. 15:4). "Pleasant words are a honeycomb, sweet to the soul and healing to the bones" (Prov. 16:24).

• *Instruction and teaching.* "The tongue of the righteous is choice silver, but the heart of the wicked is of little value. The lips of the righteous nourish many, but fools die for lack of judgment" (Prov. 10:20–21).

Proverbs also points out words of the sort we should try to eliminate from our vocabulary.

• *Flattery and deceit.* "Food gained by fraud tastes sweet to a man, but he ends up with a mouth full of gravel" (Prov. 20:17). "A malicious man disguises himself with his lips, but in his heart he harbors deceit. A lying tongue hates those it hurts, and a flattering mouth works ruin" (Prov. 26:24, 28). "He who rebukes a man will in the end gain more favor than he who has a flattering tongue" (Prov. 28:23).

• *Gossip and slander.* "He who conceals his hatred has lying lips, and whoever spreads slander is a fool" (Prov. 10:18). "With his mouth the godless destroys his neighbor, but through knowledge the righteous escape. A gossip betrays a confidence, but a trustworthy man keeps a secret" (Prov. 11:9,13). "A perverse man stirs up dissension, and a gossip separates close friends" (Prov. 16:28). "He who covers over an offense promotes love, but whoever repeats the matter separates close friends" (Prov. 17:9). "A fool's lips bring him strife, and his mouth invites a beating. A fool's mouth is his undoing, and his lips are a snare to his soul. The words of a gossip are like choice morsels; they go down to a man's inmost parts" (Prov. 18:6–8).

• *Bragging and boasting.* "Pride goes before destruction, a haughty spirit before a fall. Better to be lowly in spirit and among the oppressed than to share plunder with the proud" (Prov. 16:18–19). "Let another praise you, and not your own mouth; someone else, and not your own lips" (Prov. 27:2).

• *Vulgarity and profanity.* "Put away perversity from your mouth; keep corrupt talk far from your lips" (Prov. 4:24). "The tongue that brings healing is a tree of life, but a deceitful tongue crushes the spirit" (Prov. 15:4). "Better a poor man whose walk is blameless than a fool whose lips are perverse" (Prov. 19:1).

• *Lies and exaggeration.* "Truthful lips endure forever, but a lying tongue lasts only a moment" (Prov. 12:19). "A truthful witness saves lives, but a false witness is deceitful" (Prov. 14:25).

• *Argument and strife.* "Starting a quarrel is like breaching a dam; so drop the matter before a dispute breaks out" (Prov. 17:14). "A fool's lips bring him strife, and his mouth invites a beating" (Prov. 18:6). "An angry man stirs up dissension, and a hot-tempered one commits many sins" (Prov. 29:22).

Heeding the guidance of Proverbs helps us greatly in the lifelong challenge of taming our tongue and using it for positive influence and not negative. We can also look to contemporary sources of advice in this area. *How to Speak and How to Listen* was written by Mortimer Adler, the former chairman of the board of editors for Encyclopedia Britannica. Anyone seriously interested in trying to improve his or her logos should become a friend of this great book. In it, Adler classifies the four main types of speaking: social conversation, personal heart-to-heart talk, impersonal and theoretical talk that is instructive or enlightening, and impersonal and practical talk that is persuasive with respect to action. Within this framework, Adler offers a wealth of valuable analysis and input about shaping and giving a message.

What Makes *a* Meaningful Message?

We want to conclude with a fivefold test applicable to any messages we send as well as the ones we receive, to determine whether they are meaningful within the context of influence.

1. *Is the message true?* A meaningful message is true. As we stated in Chapter Two, honesty is a fertile field in which wisdom, and as a result influence, can grow. As was famously written in *Mark Twain's Notebook,* "All men are liars, partial or hiders of facts, half tellers of

truths, shirks, moral sneaks. When a merely honest man appears he is a comet—his fame is eternal—needs no genius, no talent—mere honesty." An honest person with a truthful message is poised to light up the sky with his influence.

2. *Is the message helpful?* A meaningful message is helpful. The central ethic of the Hippocratic Oath taken by physicians as they enter professional life is "First, do no harm." Everyone who wants to wield greater clout would do well to take the same oath. We recently worked with a friend who was wrestling through a business situation involving some difficult issues with his partner. We made the case that our friend needed to construct a line of argument in which his partner felt he was being helped, not harmed.

3. *Is the message inviting?* A meaningful message is inviting. Never underestimate the value of storytelling; it's an indispensable tool in crafting your message and sprinkling any message with invitation. It is a tool to bring your listener up close with attention. Gerry Spence, author of *How to Argue and Win Every Time,* offers this perspective on its power:

> Storytelling has been the principal means by which we have taught one another from the beginning of time. The campfire. The tribal members gathered round, the little children peeping from behind the adults, their eyes as wide as dollars, listening, listening. The old man—can you hear his crackly voice, telling his stories of days gone by? Something is learned from the story—the way to surround and kill a saber-toothed tiger, the hunt for the king of the mastodons in a far-off valley, how the old man survived the storm. There are stories of love, of the discovery of magic potions, of the evil of the warring neighboring tribes—all learning of man has been handed down for eons in the form of stories.

Storytelling has been part of the learning-and-influence highway forever. It's a way for us to invite people to lean in to hear our message, rather than away. Parents, coaches, salesmen, business executives, physicians all should make more use of the story.

4. *Is the message relevant?* A meaningful message is relevant. Most businesses, especially advertising companies, go through a transformation

every few years brought about by asking themselves some tough questions: Are we in step with people, culturally, socially, and in other ways? Do we need to adapt and adjust our message to changing needs in our audience? Similarly, in our world of influence, with the growing and graying of every generation and with other changes in our audience's experience, we must recalibrate our message for relevance.

5. *Is the message clear?* A meaningful message is clear. This question involves stepping away from our message a bit, looking at it critically, and asking if it makes sense. You may have the most brilliant idea of the century, but if you can't make people understand what you mean, the influence you could exert goes nowhere.

A good friend of mine told me not long ago about his experience in the world of vehicle purchasing and maintenance. He had bought the last four vehicles from the same dealer and was very satisfied with the cars and the service at the dealership. A national chain took over the dealership, and they saturated the market with ads and promotions. Their message was, "Come here and buy from us; you will be happy you did." My friend took his car in and to his amazement was sorely disappointed. The business was nothing but a storefront—empty promises, nonexistent service and quality. My friend sold his car immediately and never went back, and he told every friend he knew to avoid the place.

The same possibility exists in our everyday communication. Proverbs 19:18 says, "Reckless words pierce like a sword, but the words of the wise bring healing." The right words are only part of logos as a whole. It also involves our minds and our hearts and how we put ourselves into our message. We have to mine our lives for elements of value and worth, and then put those elements into our message so that our influence has a positive, meaningful, long-lasting impact. Otherwise we're simply a flashy storefront with words painted on the window and nothing inside on the shelves.

• • •

KEY POINTS

- Logos, from which we derive the word *logic,* refers to actual, literal words spoken, but also to the mind of the speaker, the structure of the argument, and the underlying reasoning used to make a point.

- An argument is only necessary if there is disagreement between the speaker and audience. To arrive at agreement out of disagreement, a common place is necessary. A common place is a beginning point for any argument over which all parties (at a minimum, speaker and audience) already agree.

- Gaining control of our words is a full-time, lifelong assignment. The tongue has disproportionate influence, is inherently unruly, and needs training.

- The Old Testament book of Proverbs gives advice regarding the right words for gaining influence, and the wrong words to avoid depleting influence. Here are the right words:

Wise counsel and sound advice

Honest feedback and caution

Encouragement and kindness

Instruction and teaching

Here are the wrong words:

Flattery and deceit

Gossip and slander

Bragging and boasting

Vulgarity and profanity

Lies and exaggeration

Argument and strife

- Not all of our daily messages measure the same in the weight of their value.

- Criteria for a meaningful message:

Is the message true?

Is it helpful?

Is it inviting?

Is it relevant?

Is it clear?

5

Pathos

An Audience That Is Receptive

You can't drive straight on a twisting lane.

—Russian Proverb

I
T'S HIGHLY UNLIKELY THAT A YOUNG MAN WOULD
casually mumble to his girlfriend while driving down the road,
"Hey, by the way, ya wanna get married?" On the contrary, he spends
weeks, even months, staging a major event, creating the perfect environment in which to ask the big question. He takes her to the lake
where they had their first date. Or they linger over a glass of wine in
an elegant restaurant with candlelit tables. Or he cleverly plants the
ring in her favorite breakfast cereal box, wrapped up with a bow of her
favorite colors. Although the question (logos) is really rather simply,
"Would you marry me" he makes sure the stage is set for a memorable
occasion—and a favorable response.

Receptivity is a key variable in the influence equation; many times
it determines whether we are in fact influential. Pathos is the role of
environment, culture, timing, and other external elements in determining an audience's receptiveness in an experience of influence. The
lovestruck young man with a ring in his pocket who goes to great

lengths in staging the situation is optimizing pathos in an effort to influence his girlfriend's answer.

There's a mysterious process that occurs in the audience (whether it's one or millions) during a potentially influential situation. They can go with you, or they can stay put. If they don't engage, it's difficult to recover. If they do, it's easy to cover up deficiencies. Take a basketball game, for example. If the crowd is on its feet, cheering, responding to what's happening on the court, the team's chances of winning are high. Noise from the crowd doesn't automatically alter the physical size of the opponent or transform our guards into mini–Kobe Bryants. But somehow, mysteriously, cheering fans play an important role in the outcome of the game, in the players' "persuasiveness." Just ask the coaches. Or look at the win-loss record for home games versus away games.

The same is true in a speaking situation. If you can get your audience to participate, to engage with you, whether wittingly or unwittingly, you increase pathos tremendously. We see this process at work in any situation where a speaker—whether a teacher, a seminar leader, or even a writer—asks the audience a question and waits for an answer. A writer might say, "Put this book down for a few moments and jot down five things you've noticed about this topic." Or a businesswoman making a presentation flashes PowerPoint slides on the wall that illuminate her most important points. The idea is to engage the audience members' imagination, to direct their thoughts along a certain track, to get them to enter into your argument with you.

Incidentally, the concept of pathos is part of what set Aristotle apart from other teachers of influence. His claim that part of the process of persuasiveness, or influence, rested on the audience was unique. I saw pathos clearly illustrated when I taught a class at the University of Arkansas. One particular student would show up to class, sit in the back, pile his books on his desk, put his head on his books, and promptly fall asleep. This happened regularly, and it killed the class. Giving the lecture was like trying to drive with a flat tire. Finally, one day I approached the student after class and said, "Look. If you want to sleep, you need to leave. And if you leave, please don't come back." The student left my class and never showed up again. The effect on classroom dynamics was immediate and profound. Students were more attentive, they participated in discussion more enthusiastically, and the overall atmosphere was much more alive. My message (logos) and my credibility (ethos) were unchanged. But a change in pathos made all the difference.

Many elements come into play with pathos. Most people in sales are expert at setting the stage for a buyer to say yes, whether it's by playing golf, taking a client to dinner, sending a gift, or offering tickets to the Super Bowl. A similar thought process goes into planning an annual meeting for a major corporation. The event, ostensibly to offer information about the previous and coming years for the company, turns into a massive celebration full of celebrities and cultural heroes. Food, carnival rides, activities for children, and musicians may all be on hand. The idea is to use pathos to support the logos that the CEO or chairman is about to lay out for the stockholders.

In Aristotle's day, pathos referred to an intense emotional experience between a speaker and audience. The definition is relevant today, but it also extends well beyond the speaker-audience context. It can take place between anyone, individuals or groups, where one party is trying to persuade the other. It's where we get our word *apathetic* (the prefix *a-* means *without*), which is definitely not what we want in the pursuit of greater, more intentional influence.

READING *the* TEA LEAVES

There is an ancient myth that says some people are able to look into a teacup and read the future from the pattern formed by the tea leaves on the bottom of the cup. We don't put much stock in this, but it is a terrific picture of setting one's radar to read the environment for key indicators. In our journey toward greater influence, we have to peer into an influence situation and read the pathos. Here are some of the pathos elements we have to be aware of.

Timing

I was asked to speak one summer at a national conference in a stadium filled with people. My time slot was Saturday afternoon at 1:45 P.M.— right after lunch. This group of people had been up late the night before and risen early that morning, and when I got up to speak you might as well have pulled out cots and sleeping bags and played a soft lullaby over the PA system. Everything but the cookies and warm milk were staged for an afternoon snooze. Needless to say, timing was a key factor in my influence strategy.

It is timing that restricts my wife and me from having a serious conversation about kids, work, or money late at night. We have learned the hard way. At the end of an exhausting day, to begin an already challenging conversation at ten-thirty doesn't work; at least for us it doesn't. The pathos tea leaves are reading loud and clear, "Don't do it; wait." The book of Proverbs contains a rather humorous observation on this topic: "If a man loudly blesses his neighbor early in the morning, it will be taken as a curse" (27:14). Even good news, like receiving a gift at two-thirty in the morning, isn't seen as good. The right timing can make all the difference.

Environment

At another conference in Florida a number of years ago, I spoke to a room full of people. Although the timing was much better, the setting and environment were much worse. The conference room was long and shotgun-style; each row contained barely twelve people across. For some reason, the floor sloped down from where I was standing instead of up, and when the sound system wasn't garbling and distorting my words, it was emitting ear-piercing screeches and whines. Again, not my most effective moment as a speaker. (Now I always ask questions of pathos on the front end.)

On a similar note, a boss who gets out from behind her desk to sit in a chair next to an employee for a significant conversation is hoping to adjust the pathos "thermostat." Or a parent might take a challenging teenager out for ice cream to talk through some touchy issues that are on the mind of the parent and should be on the mind of the wild teen. The logistical circumstances are important to the outcome of an influence situation.

Weather

The literal weather—rain, sun, wind, fog, humidity—often comes to bear on a situation. The amount of time we spend talking about weather and watching it on television sometimes borders on the ridiculous. But part of our fascination with the weather is due to its potential to affect outcomes. We attended an outdoor wedding the other day; outdoor weddings are always risky. The day was supposed to be extremely hot, and the mosquitoes were at their summer peak. Two hours before the wedding, the sky opened and the rain brought Niagara Falls to us. You want the waterfall on the honeymoon, not on the afternoon of an outside wedding! The tenseness over the wedding party was palpable; I'd never seen so many grim faces. But the rainstorm passed, leaving the air cool, clear, and mosquito-free. The wedding was perfect, and almost every face was smiling. Nothing changed except the weather.

Recently, I was in New York City with my wife for a brief getaway weekend that rolled into a couple of work days for me. Although we had planned a fun-filled time, we kept an eye on the weather channel. Why? Three days in New York City (or on a Florida beach) can be dramatically altered by the weather.

Other Players

Part of the service we provide at Cornerstone Group, our consulting firm, is strategic life coaching. It involves our working alongside an executive, helping sort out some personal and professional issues. When we provide this kind of service, we refuse to take on a client who has another life coach. Nor in our consulting business will we take on someone who has another consultant. Why? We have learned through two decades of consulting that when too many people whisper into the chief's ear, problems are inevitable. It's like a pilot getting multiple signals on where to land from the air traffic control tower.

It is a good thing to have multiple counselors, according to Proverbs. But I don't think the wise writer of Proverbs was suggesting that everyone shout out their wisdom and counsel all at the same time.

Sometimes an employee sets up a meeting and requests that certain other people be present in the room because of the impact they are likely to have on the situation. Or they might ask that certain people not attend, for exactly the same reason. Other players can detract from or enhance our influence greatly.

Pathos is the element of the influence triangle that I am least in control of. I can sometimes make adjustments in a situation, but I must largely accept the circumstances as they are and do my best to work within the environment. I can be like the Indian from old cartoons with his ear to the ground listening for what's approaching and his finger in the air to determine the direction of the wind. I look for signals in the environment to direct me which way to go.

If I'm delivering bad news, I need to think about pathos. If I'm delivering good news, I need to think about pathos. If I'm trying to persuade someone to say yes or no, I need to think about pathos.

The EXPERIENCE ECONOMY

Is pathos really that important, you ask? In 1999, an excellent book was introduced: *The Experience Economy,* by Joseph Pine and James Gilmore. Their thesis is that work is theater and every business is a stage. Essentially, they build the case that our society has been transformed, step by step. At one time, commodities were the basis of our economy. Then it became goods, then services. But now, they propose, the ultimate business transaction is the sale and purchase of experience. The seller in the commodity environment was the trader, in goods it was the manufacturer, and in services it was the provider; in experience, the seller is a stager.

A restaurant is a place not just to get a meal but to experience a theme with music, special lighting, and sound effects. A company's annual meeting is no longer about information only but about food, rides, and fun. Websites are no longer just informational; they contain games and conversations and even community. Some businesses, such as Disney, fit this model inherently, but it's bigger than that. Saturn and Starbucks, for example, construct an experience for customers that goes beyond cars and coffee. The offering of experiences is changing how we do business and expect business to be done.

According to Pine and Gilmore, "Experiences represent an existing but previously unarticulated genre of economic output. Recognizing experiences as a distinct economic offering provides the key to future economic growth" (pages 9–10). If their theories are correct—and we believe they have been and will continue to be proved true—the pathos component is critical. An experience involves environment, timing, and weather—all the things we've talked about with pathos. Weaving these elements together to orchestrate a certain response in an individual is what the experience economy and pathos entail.

The MANY FACES *of* RESISTANCE

A major part of pathos is group dynamics, which can be greatly affected by individuals. One high-maintenance person who consumes the majority of your energy or one naysayer who sees only negative possibilities can sabotage your attempt to influence. On the other hand, one enthusiast on the team can be a launching pad for success. Jim Collins, author of *Good to Great,* refers to this concept when he discusses a company's need to get the wrong people off the bus and the right people on the bus if it's going to achieve greatness.

This concept also involves corporate culture and its significance in a company's success. When Wal-Mart was going through its first generational transition from Sam Walton to David Glass, a predominant question in everyone's mind was the maintenance of culture. As Wal-Mart moved forward, would the company maintain its culture, its pathos, which was such a real element of success? The company asked our friend, Don Soderquist, to be the keeper of the culture; he did a marvelous job of transmitting the heritage and values of the last generation to the new generation.

Not long ago, I was standing in front of an airline ticket counter needing to change airlines. This process is difficult enough with a paid ticket, but I was using frequent flyer miles on this trip, and it seemed I was asking for the impossible. Standing in front of me was a ticket agent, and everything about her face said no. It was a battle-worn face of rejection and resistance. Recognizing this face is an important part of pathos. Much of influence and clout involves getting someone to say yes even if the person is hard-wired to say no. Or the opposite can be true. You may need for someone to say no when they want to say yes—a small sole proprietor who just can't refuse a sale, for instance. But usually it's the no face on the other side of the counter.

There are several faces of rejection and resistance, and recognizing them is the first step toward getting them to become a face of acceptance and willingness.

• *Firm, mean defiance.* This is a solid, entrenched no. Parents see it in their kids; kids see it in their parents. It can also come up between students and teachers, bosses and employees. We all have seen the face of firm, mean defiance and resistance at one time or another.

• *Wobbly, nice resistance.* In this model of resistance, someone seems kind and polite, almost as if the person is agreeing with you, but the answer is still no. You may not even realize it's a no at the time. But it is.

• *Eternal, indefinite stalling.* We don't want to be too hard on the airlines, but they are notorious for this kind of resistance. You wait and wait, leaving message after message, but you never get an answer. Finally, by default, the answer is no. The restaurant industry is also known for this kind of resistance. They do not tell you there is a two-hour wait; rather, they "twenty minutes" you to death. People who sell advertising are familiar with encountering this kind of resistance from a prospect.

• *Jackrabbit—quick enthusiasm that fades quickly.* In Chapter One we talked about Jesus' parable of the sower who scatters seed on several kinds of soil. One handful of seed falls into shallow soil and shoots up quickly, but it withers as soon as the first noonday sun hits it. This is the kind of person we're talking about here—someone who buys in too quickly, without any thought or foresight, and then has no staying power to see the conclusion through. There's no rootedness in this person.

These are some of the common faces of no that we encounter. But there are more. There is a resistance that's like an elephant: it's not really intentionally resistant, it's just a huge animal that requires a great push to get it moving. Many people in corporate life face this kind of resistance. No one is really saying no to their ideas or enthusiasm, but a huge corporation doesn't change quickly or easily. Then there's a house-cat reaction. It may seem fierce and even wild in its resistance, but it's not really dangerous, just playful. Finally, there's the resistance of a snake—it will bite you, and it means business. Approach and handle with great caution.

The distinction between the face and the characteristic of resistance is important. If we're going to learn how to influence people correctly, whether through small verbal transactions or a campaign of many years, we need to realize that not everyone has a hand in the air, saying, "Please influence me." There are few people like that. Many members of our audience are on the opposite side of the influence experience, and their resistance to change is entirely natural.

USING PATHOS *for* ADVANTAGE—BUT *with* CAUTION

Some years back, we traveled to the Pacific Northwest for a meeting—specifically, someone was pitching us an idea. Our meeting was held on a very nice boat that puttered around the Seattle harbor, where we could smell the salt air, see the glittering city against a backdrop of mountains, and dine on fresh seafood. Obviously, our host was pulling out all the stops to use pathos to advantage. Everything was in place for a favorable response from us.

Another example: I heard a student leader speak to parents of teenagers, saying, "Do you want to get your kids to talk? Then take them out to eat, or put food in front of them." His point, though he didn't state it this way, was that if you orchestrate the pathos, the logos goes better.

However, we must be careful not to over-rely on pathos. In today's business world, much is changing. Our office is in northwest Arkansas, which also happens to be home to the Wal-Mart headquarters. For years, we traveled on planes with salespeople from all over the country. Wal-Mart is a plum market for any company's products, and on those planes are the best salespeople you will find when it comes to making the pitch and sealing the deal. They come to Wal-Mart at the top of their class, wearing designer suits and carrying a briefcase full of persuasion strategies.

Then they arrive at the Northwest Arkansas Airport. It's in the country, and they can't get a cab. They check in at a hotel that's clean but simple, not the five-star variety where they can whip out their card and get VIP treatment. The day of the meeting, they go to the Wal-Mart home office and meet a young buyer, who is likely to be wearing a wrinkled shirt and crooked tie. Instead of a lavish conference room with plush leather chairs and a mahogany table, they sit on metal folding chairs in a room that looks like a jail cell and is not much bigger. If the salesperson offers to buy lunch, sneak some cigars under the table, or treat for a round of golf, the buyer says no. He's not allowed to accept anything from a product salesperson.

If the salesperson doesn't have a strong case, he's out of luck. The world is moving to an experience economy, and Wal-Mart wants *its customers* to have the full low-price experience in retail. But when it comes to its own purchasing, Wal-Mart wants to "de-pathos" the transaction, or at least stack the pathos to its own advantage rather than the seller's.

We use this example in closing to illustrate that pathos on its own falls short of being truly influential. Without a clear, substantive message (logos) and strong integrity (ethos, which we'll talk about in the next chapter), pathos is merely illusion. Environment can enhance influence, but all the ambience in the world can't disguise a weak message or faulty character forever. Without all three legs of Aristotle's Triangle in place, you don't have a triangle; it's just an incomplete image that doesn't mean anything.

• • •

Key Points

- The receptivity of our message (pathos) with our audience often determines whether or not we are influential.
- You increase pathos tremendously when you can get your audience to participate, wittingly or unwittingly, in your presentation.
- Elements to consider in dealing with pathos:

  Timing

  Environment

  Weather

  Other players
- The current experience economy driving business and life heightens the need to interpret pathos and use it advantageously.
- Faces of resistance and rejection:

  Firm, mean resistance

  Wobbly, nice resistance

  Eternal, indefinite stalling

  Jackrabbit—quick enthusiasm that fades quickly
- Environment can enhance influence, but all the ambience in the world can't disguise a weak message or faulty character forever

Ethos

A Life That Is Believable

Character is much better kept than recovered.

—Thomas Paine

B EFORE THE SUMMER OF 2002, JOHN RIGAS WAS
considered an unimpeachable elder statesman of the business community and a generous public benefactor. He was a World War II veteran. He graduated from a modest but respected polytechnic institute
in New York state. He founded a small cable television company in
Coudersport, Pennsylvania, with his brother, built it into a national
corporation, and kept the business local and family-controlled. He
named the company Adelphia, from the Greek word for *brother,* to
symbolize commitment to family and customer service.

Rigas's apparent dedication to western New York, where he grew
up, and northern Pennsylvania, where Adelphia was based, drew admiration from the media and loyalty from those who benefited from
his active community involvement. In 1998, Rigas was named entrepreneur of the year by his alma mater. In 2001, the *Buffalo News* called
him the city's most powerful and influential business leader because
of his ownership of the Buffalo Sabres hockey team and investment

in the development of downtown. He was a member of the Rotary Club and served on numerous boards.

But then the illusion began to crack apart. In May 2002, Rigas resigned as chairman of Adelphia. In June, the company filed for bankruptcy. In July, he and his two sons were awakened from their beds and arrested by federal agents on conspiracy charges. Rigas was accused of having used company money as his personal piggy bank to buy the Sabres hockey team, a golf course, real estate, and private jets, and hiding $2.3 billion in liabilities from investors. All told, the loss to Adelphia stockholders was estimated at $60 billion. The respectable, generous businessman was gone, and in his place was a broken-down and defeated swindler being led away in handcuffs on national television.

Rigas's arrest occurred amid a rash of corporate scandal that rocked Wall Street and dismayed the public. Report after report revealed that company leaders who were responsible for guarding investor and employee interests were playing fast and loose with that trust. Enron. Arthur Andersen. ImClone. WorldCom. The image of personal integrity, for the leaders of these companies and more, crumbled or was seriously shaken, over and over again.

What was so remarkable about these events, beyond the astonishing abuse of trust, was the revelation that a person could turn out to be so different from the image he or she presented. But the practice of displaying a chosen image isn't limited to a corporate top dog. As human beings, we all go to great lengths to construct a quality of truthfulness around what we say and who we claim to be. As kids, we "cross my heart and hope to die, stick a needle in my eye" if we don't do what we say we will. As adults we swear on the Bible, on our mother's grave, by Jove, and so on to underline that what we say is true. We strive to reinforce the perception that we're believable; the more bizarre the oath, the more likely we are to keep it, or so the logic seems to go.

An Ancient Tradition

This almost mystical ritual has been around for a long time. Down through the years, an oath has generally followed the same formula: a speaker makes a solemn declaration or pledge and appeals to God or some other supernatural force for an affirmation of truthfulness. This process was especially common in Old Testament times. As the nation and culture of Israel evolved, the ancient Hebrews developed an elaborate system of underscoring their promises. In His communication with His chosen people, God emphasized the importance of keeping these pledges. Numbers 30:2 says, "When a man makes a vow to the Lord or takes an oath to obligate himself by a pledge, he must not break his word but must do everything he said." Leviticus 19:12 warns, "Do not swear falsely by my name and so profane the name of your God. I am the Lord." An oath before the Lord was not something to treat casually.

But even when vows were treated with the seriousness God demanded, the concept of the oath gave way to the idea of degrees of truthfulness. People began compartmentalizing God's influence—heaven, the earth, Jerusalem, and even one's own hair symbolized different aspects of God's involvement in life. Each aspect of God could be attached, like a magic rabbit foot, to a statement to lend a certain degree of credibility to the one making the oath, as if the statement itself were not strong enough to stand on its own. We see the same process at work today in children (and some adults) who cross their hearts and hope to die when they declare something to be true.

Fast forward to the New Testament and Jesus' Sermon on the Mount in Matthew 5. In this address, Christ turns the Jewish religious code upside down by painting a radical and startling word picture of the heavenly kingdom. Remember Aristotle's common place, the strategy of finding something shared with your audience and using that as the starting point for your argument? Jesus used the technique masterfully. In the Sermon on the Mount, Jesus brings up religious teachings familiar to everyone in His audience regarding murder, adultery, divorce, revenge, enemies—and truthfulness. You can almost see the heads nodding in the crowd. But time after time, He spins His listeners around to a whole new perspective, and now you can see the confused faces. He guides His followers from an external, showy, public outlook on religion to a faith that is from the heart, grown from the inside out. Over and over, He tells those gathered around Him, "You've heard it this way all your lives, but I'm going to reconstruct your belief system from the ground up."

Part of this address to His early followers hits on the subject of oaths and truthfulness.

> Again, you have heard that it was said to the people long ago, 'Do not break your oath, but keep the oaths you have made to the Lord.' But I tell you, Do not swear at all: either by heaven, for it is God's throne; or by the earth, for it is his footstool; or by Jerusalem, for it is the city of the Great King. And do not swear by your head, for you cannot make even one hair white or black. Simply let your 'Yes' be 'Yes,' and your 'No,' 'No'; anything beyond this comes from the evil one [Matt. 5:33–37].

The clear conclusion is that people who make casual commitments and offhand remarks ought to treat those statements with the same kind of sincerity and solemnity as they would an official oath. Jesus lifts all conversation to the level of binding: ego-boosting exaggeration, a casual promise, flippancy in sacred things, sharp retaliation, inappropriate humor and sarcasm, and so on. Contrary to the central concept of the ancient oath-making tradition, there are not degrees of truth. A yes is a yes, and a no is a no, plain and simple. Elaborate attempts to enhance and distinguish our truthful statements from the rest of our speech are not only ineffective but originate from the enemy of truth and lead us down a destructive path. The speech of a follower of Jesus should be plain, clear, and straightforward.

Yet if we shun the surface symbols of truth as empty and harmful, what puts the stamp of truthfulness on our speech, our action, our lives? If we seek to be an effective influence in our world, how do we convey that we are trustworthy? The answer is simple and tremendously complex: character. In a time of falsehood, half-truths, and broken commitments, someone with true clout is easily recognized by believability in who he is; the outer appearance matches the inner person.

A BELIEVABLE LIFE

Aristotle referred to the believability of someone's life as her ethos. Words that are related in meaning and concept are ethics, credibility, character, and integrity. In a specifically rhetorical context, ethos involves the audience's perception of the person giving a speech or making an argument: does that person's life match her message? It involves the process of an audience member asking, "How do I know if I can believe what this person is saying? What is it about her, either from what I know of her life (antecedent ethos) or in how she's coming across right now (immediate ethos), that puts weight behind what she's telling me?" The answer to those questions determines whether the speaker's ethos is high, allowing her to be influential, or low, which undercuts her clout severely.

The same questions apply in a broader context as we attempt to be influential not just in speeches and arguments but in the very nature of how we live our lives. If people perceive a hypocritical gap between who we claim to be and who we really are, we might as well throw in the influence towel because we have no game when it comes to building clout or making a meaningful impact on other people. In fact, inauthenticity often produces the opposite effect of what we hoped for. People tend to run in the opposite direction from the destination we advocate if they see deceit and hypocrisy in us.

Aristotle made the case, and we wholeheartedly support it, that in the three-stranded cord of logos, pathos, and ethos, ethos carries the strongest connection to influence and persuasion. Sometimes this is hard to believe because we see people all the time who say one thing and do another but seem to hold terrific influence. However, if we were able to see the results of their influence in the long run, we might get another perspective. A coach who smokes but tells his players to avoid tobacco products might take his team to the championships, but his superb coaching might foolishly end early because of his physical health. Parents who have regular shouting matches but tell their children to practice self-control are setting a dangerous tone for their children's future relationships. A boss who tells her employees to practice ethical business conduct but then dips into the till and fudges the books is leaving herself wide open to embezzlement and dishonesty. It's the conduct of our lives in the quiet moments, out of the spotlight, when we think no one is looking, that determines our influence in the long run.

INTERNAL MOORINGS

So, where does a life of believability, of character and integrity, start? The short answer is that it starts in the heart. All the things that make a person believable originate in the heart. I started thinking about this subject seriously and intentionally after one of those flash-bulb moments that will always be printed on my mind as a turning point in life. This is what happened.

Several years ago, as part of my ongoing effort to be an active, involved father (which I hope I always strive to be), I made a date with my daughter Julianne to escort her to gymnastics practice. After practice, we had agreed to have a special lunch together. There was just one condition: little brother Kile, my youngest, was coming along. We made a deal that we'd baby-sit him together.

So we went to the gymnastics studio and I pulled my chair up to the sidelines. I didn't start dialing my cell phone, reading the paper, or going over my to-do list as was often the case; instead I focused on the bouncy ball of energy out on the floor with blond hair and blue eyes that carried my same last name. My goal for the next sixty minutes was that every time those two blue eyes looked at me, my own two blue eyes would say something back to her.

As I was thus engaged, I didn't notice Kile exploring the trash on the floor, until he was standing in front of me with a Tootsie Pop in his hand—in his three-year-old judgment, the reward for his labors. The wrapper was in place but not perfectly snug, and I could hear my wife's voice saying, "Are you kidding me? It was on the *floor.*" So, to Kile's heartbreak, I denied him the Tootsie Pop. The instructor overheard our exchange and her heart went out to Kile, so she walked into her office, to the mother lode, the source of all Tootsie Pops. She reemerged with a five-gallon jar and let Kile take his pick. I said OK, but he had to wait until after lunch to eat it.

With that, my three-year-old and I commenced the battle. He wanted it now; I said wait. He said yes; I said no. He asked why; I said because I said so. He didn't give up, and I didn't give up. Finally, amid much weeping and gnashing of teeth, he gave in. Off to lunch we went. We walked into a local restaurant and saw our good friends Gary and Ann out on a Saturday date. As we stopped to say hello, Kile marched up to the couple (whom he didn't know very well at all), thrust his hard-won sucker up to their faces, and said, "I get to eat this right after lunch."

The reaction was immediate. "Oooh, aaaah," they said, looking down at Kile. "To be able to wait, that's so good. You have such a strong heart." And they patted his little chest as they continued to ooh and aah over his strong heart.

My brain came to a screeching standstill. You see, I thought they would say to Kile, "What patience," or "What self-control you have." That's what they were supposed to say, but they didn't. They said, "What a strong heart." It made quite an impression on Kile, and also on his dad. Since that day, I've been filtering and studying life through the lens of what it means to have a strong heart.

There are more than a thousand verses in the Bible that mention the heart. Just one of them is Proverbs 27:19, which says, "As water reflects a face, so a man's heart reflects the man." Obviously, the writers are not referring to the physical organ that pumps blood through our bodies. The word *heart* refers to the seat of the inner human, the control instrument that directs the whole person. The heart contains desires, feelings, intellect, the will, the ability to set principles, and morality. It's the inner element around which the package of blood, bones, and skin is sewn. The heart is our internal mooring, and it is where important things happen. Here is a list of some of these processes, according to Scripture. The heart is where we

PROCESS LIFE

In his heart a man plans his course, but the Lord determines his steps. (Proverbs 16:9)

Then I thought in my heart, "The fate of the fool will overtake me also. What then do I gain by being wise?" I said in my heart, "This too is meaningless." For the wise man, like the fool, will not be long remembered; in days to come both will be forgotten. Like the fool, the wise man too must die! So my heart began to despair over all my toilsome labor under the sun. (Ecclesiastes 2:15, 16, 20)

PONDER ETERNITY

He has made everything beautiful in its time. He has also set eternity in the hearts of men; yet they cannot fathom what God has done from beginning to end. (Ecclesiastes 3:11)

TRANSMIT HERITAGE TO OUR CHILDREN

He will turn the hearts of the fathers to their children, and the hearts of the children to their fathers; or else I will come and strike the land with a curse. (Malachi 4:6)

ENGAGE IN REAL WORSHIP

These people come near to me with their mouth and honor me with their lips, but their hearts are far from me. Their worship of me is made up only of rules taught by men. (Isaiah 29:13)

Speak to one another with psalms, hymns and spiritual songs. Sing and make music in your heart to the Lord. (Ephesians 5:19)

FILTER NEGATIVE EMOTION

How I hated discipline! How my heart spurned correction! (Proverbs 5:12)

Peace I leave with you; my peace I give you. I do not give to you as the world gives. Do not let your hearts be troubled and do not be afraid. (John 14:27)

CONQUER SIN CYCLES

"Are you so dull?" he asked. "Don't you see that nothing that enters a man from the outside can make him 'unclean'? For it doesn't go into his heart but into his stomach, and then out of his body." (In saying this, Jesus declared all foods "clean.") He went on: "What comes out of a man is what makes him 'unclean.' For from within, out of men's hearts, come evil thoughts, sexual immorality, theft, murder, adultery, greed, malice, deceit, lewdness, envy, slander, arrogance and folly. All these evils come from inside and make a man 'unclean.'" (Mark 7:18–23)

Repent of this wickedness and pray to the Lord. Perhaps he will forgive you for having such a thought in your heart. (Acts 8:22–23)

MAKE DECISIONS

Listen, my son, and be wise, and keep your heart on the right path. (Proverbs 23:19)

KNIT FRIENDSHIPS

It is right for me to feel this way about all of you, since I have you in my heart; for whether I am in chains or defending and confirming the gospel, all of you share in God's grace with me. (Philippians 1:7)

COMMUNICATE WITH GOD

For it is with your heart that you believe and are justified, and it is with your mouth that you confess and are saved. (Romans 10:10)

FORGE GOOD CHARACTER

Wisdom reposes in the heart of the discerning and even among fools she lets herself be known. (Proverbs 14:33)

Turn my heart toward your statutes and not toward selfish gain. (Psalm 119:36)

A heart filled with truthfulness, honesty, and virtue results in a believable person. Oftentimes, the construction of this kind of life is unseen and private. My friend Gary (the same Gary who commended my son for his strong heart) recently built his dream house on a beautiful piece of land outside of town. In northwest Arkansas, the high water table and a network of underground caves, springs, and rocks make building construction a challenge, to say the least. Gary was determined to avoid the foundation trouble that had plagued his previous two houses, so he poured twenty-three "helix piers" into the ground, a complex, costly, and time-consuming process. Gary and his wife spent a huge portion of their budget on the foundation—a hidden, unseen part of the house. But the result was a foundation that supported their house above the shifting, treacherous earth below. Likewise, the construction of the heart is a critical component of building a believable life that takes abundant energy and extensive resources. We don't just happen to acquire a strong heart. We have to cultivate it.

Although we're taking the basis of our thoughts about the heart from Scripture, this is not a foreign concept in the business world. In fact, in our experience most investment meetings include a session in which potential investors quiz company leaders about their personal lives. These investors realize that they are not funding an idea, but a person. There is an assumption in the investment community that a person who is going to take the money and run with the idea ought to be believable and trustworthy.

BELIEVABLE BUT *not* PERFECT

Despite the value and emphasis we're placing on good character, we want to stress that believability does not equal perfection. We all fall short, trip, make mistakes, and stub our toe. But even failure can enhance believability if we are authentic and transparent in handling our mistakes rather than being deceptive, elusive, and assigning blame. My son recently missed a question on a test for which he'd studied long and hard. At home he double-checked his answer and found that he had indeed given the correct response. He spoke with his teacher, who agreed that she had made a mistake when grading his test. She even wrote a note apologizing for the error. We posted that apology note in our kitchen. Why? To drill down a helix pier point: that everyone makes mistakes. If the third grade teacher makes a mistake and apologizes, then we all need to. This was an important lesson for my son, who has shown some perfectionist tendencies—that everyone slips up sometimes and the important issue is how we handle our mistakes, not avoiding them altogether.

Now, we realize that some people tend to apologize quickly for their misdeeds to settle the waters but have no intention of altering their behavior. We're not talking about that kind of approach, which is simply another form of dishonesty and a sure way to undermine someone's trust in us. But a genuine mistake in the context of an honest life should not harm our character. Believability and perfection are not the same.

In our attempt to construct a believable life, there are some simple truths about failure that we should keep in the forefront of our mind:

- In the course of a life journey, we make mistakes. Perfection is not the goal; trust and believability are.

- Learning to handle failure correctly means accepting it without excuse and rationalization. We must learn the magic of "I'm sorry," "I made a mistake," "I failed," and "It was my fault."

- A single failure can't be allowed to totally wipe out our self-image and confidence.

- We can learn to distinguish between a single failure and a pattern of failure and react appropriately.

- Failure can be a motivation for improvement.

- We must fix our eyes forward, not backward.

Not only is perfection impossible to attain, perfectionism can actually erode our believability and the clout we're attempting to build. This process is subtle and insidious, but it can be incredibly destructive. Back in the 1800s, the Missouri River was a prevalent route for travel and transportation of cargo between the more developed eastern states and the western frontier. The development of the steamship only increased the popularity of river travel. As more and more boats steamed up and down the Missouri, the demand for fuel increased as well. A number of riverfront entrepreneurs made a nice income cutting down trees along the banks of the Missouri and selling wood to the steamship owners. But as the trees came down, the riverbanks crumbled, making the already shallow channel even wider and shallower. In addition, trees that hadn't been cut down were no longer supported by the soil, and they toppled into the river, where they lurked treacherously below the surface, waiting to pierce the hull of an unfortunate ship traveling upstream. More than two hundred steamships have sunk in the Missouri River as the result of erosion.

The same thing can happen with our credibility: we participate in behavior that erodes our integrity and even causes damage in the lives of people we would like to influence. If we try to present a blameless, perfect image to the people around us, first of all no one believes it, and second it is impossible for anyone to identify with us. In addition to perfectionism, a number of actions can erode our trust and believability.

One is *professional doublespeak.* We have a good friend, George, who has had to learn to interpret the language of his boss. This boss has made an art form out of saying one thing but meaning another and has actually created an entire code system that is a language unto itself. Unfortunately, many people in business have learned how to do this. They say, "Let's think about this"; it really means "No way are we going to do this."

Another character-eroding behavior is holding to private (or sometimes not-so-private) *double standards.* James Kouzes and Barry Posner, in *The Leadership Challenge,* call this the DWYSYWD prescription: do what you say you will do. They write, "Credibility is mostly about consistency between words and deeds. People listen to the words and look at the deeds. Then they measure the congruence. A judgment of 'credible' is handed down when the two are consonant."

This is reminiscent of the preacher who expounds on humility but reeks with the odor of pride. It's the boss who says to watch the expenses and then always upgrades to first class. Any serious disconnect between words and action undermines credibility.

A third way to undercut our character is the *crawdad maneuver:* wiggling our way out of a difficult situation. My son and I love to explore the creeks of Arkansas. We load up our dog and drive out to one of the many clear creeks that cross through our region. The first activity is always to get wet and muddy, which is followed by some serious rock turning, looking for slippery crawdads. Catching them isn't easy because they swim backwards. One second they're under your hand, and the next they're gone in a cloud of silt. Many of us have coworkers or even bosses who conveniently shoot backwards from a conversation or tough situation. One minute they are there, then whoosh, they're gone. They have developed the art of slipping out when the heat is on. We may even have a tendency to do this ourselves. Every time we do, we lose a measure of believability.

Another way to erode integrity is to be *Mr. I Do No Wrong.* This is a person—often a perfectionist—who "never" makes a mistake and refuses to say "I'm sorry" or "Forgive me."

Lastly, we have *Ms. Empty Overcommitment.* One of the most important aspects of a life of "promise made, promise kept" is learning to filter the appropriate and the possible before responding to a request. Some of us struggle with a seeming inability to say no, and for us discerning our capacity and ability is the first step. The second step is to reserve enough emotional and physical resources to follow through on the commitment to the end. How long does a surgeon keep your trust if she schedules your surgery but has to keep postponing it because of constant overbooking? Or a restaurant that takes your reservation but can seat only half your party? Probably not very long in either case. We also need to learn to say no and yes correctly.

On the other hand, if I want to build a life of believability I must not only avoid the negative but also seek out a positive course of action. This means I must keep my stated and implied promises. How do I do this?

- By doing the right thing over and over
- By doing the right thing, especially under pressure and when it is not easy or popular
- By doing the right thing even if I'm the only one doing it
- By doing the right thing in small, private, and hidden matters
- By doing the right thing after doing the wrong thing; I admit mistakes and ask forgiveness

In Search of Ethics

Tom Peters and Robert Waterman's *In Search of Excellence,* with its highly readable and engaging language, presented the common attributes of forty-three successful American businesses. The book became a runaway bestseller in 1984 and ignited the management guru industry that continues today. Well, it's time for a business best-seller trend called *In Search of Ethics.* We seem to need it, judging by the recent run of corporate scandal, which has brought national cynicism to a high and confidence to a low.

Self-evaluation sometimes makes us uncomfortable precisely because it shines a light on some of the dark corners of ethical compromise in which many of us have participated. To illuminate and start cleaning out those corners, we need to build character and integrity, which are built on virtue. A friend of ours, Rick Sparkman, acquired a $50 million company a few years ago. Everything about the acquisition was going fine except the cultural integration, which was the result of a disconnect between Rick's ethical principles and the way the company had previously been run. So he was trying to build in virtue. We asked how he did it, and he answered with a story.

Rick would call an employee into his office and then make up an excuse to leave the room briefly. On a corner of the desk was a twenty-dollar bill. The employee didn't know it, but Rick was watching. Some employees would pick up the bill and slip it into a pocket. Some would visibly struggle but leave the bill where it was. Some saw it but didn't even glance a second time—they knew the money didn't belong to them, and that was the end of it. These employees, Rick concluded, had trained their hearts toward rightness, virtue, and integrity, and he placed trust and responsibility with them.

Right now there is widespread skepticism toward the Fortune 500, and by association with the business world in general. We need more leaders like Rick Sparkman to engage in deep and serious commitment to ethics. This is not a time to simply ignore the shipwrecked Enrons and Arthur Andersens on the beach. Any company sailing blindly ahead thinking it has no problems with integrity and ethics is headed for a wreck of its own. It's time to slow down; pull back on the throttle; and put some intense, earnest, personal effort into the ethos factor. In essence, corporate ethos is simply a magnification of the personal ethos of its employees and leaders, which means it comes down to individual commitment.

Individual commitment to a life that's believable is the key ingredient to effective influence, whether you're the leader of a billion-dollar company, a high school teacher, or the pastor of a small country church. If what we naturally do flows out of what we naturally believe, that's when lives change—our own and those around us.

• • •

Key Points

- Aristotle referred to the believability of someone's life as his or her ethos. Words that are related to it in meaning and concept include ethics, credibility, character, and integrity.
- People tend to run in the opposite direction if they see deceit and hypocrisy in us.

- It is the conduct of our lives in the quiet moments, out of the spotlight and when we think no one is looking, that determines our influence in the long run.

- All things that make a person believable originate in the heart. The heart is where we:

Process life

Ponder eternity

Transmit heritage to our children

Engage in real worship

Filter negative emotion

Conquer sin cycles

Make decisions

Knit friendships

Communicate with God

Forge good character

- Good ethos does not mean we have to be perfect, but we should avoid:

Doublespeak

Double standards

The crawdad maneuver of wiggling our way out of a difficult situation

Empty overcommitment

- My ethos is dependent upon my keeping stated and implied promises.

A Pinch of Salt
and a Ray of Light

Jesus on Influence

Love and a cough cannot be hid.

—George Herbert

EVERY WEEKEND, MY LOCAL NEWSPAPER PUBLISHES a front-page article profiling an influential person who lives in northwest Arkansas. The article dominates the paper, taking almost the entire first page and copious space inside. The story offers a glimpse into the personal life of the subject, answering questions readers might ask if given the opportunity. I have come to know many individuals through reading these stories—people I may never meet, among them surgeons, coaches, CEOs, professors, politicians, stay-at-home moms and dads, artists, attorneys, and many others.

Each profile is accompanied by a sidebar article that asks a question such as, "Who would your fantasy dinner be with?" or, "If you could sit on a park bench and visit with anyone for an hour, who would it be?" I can't count the number of times I have seen the answer "Jesus Christ."

Sometimes it seems like the right answer. Other times I read it and wonder, *Why?*

You see, not all these people would claim the Christian faith or even call themselves religious. Some are most certainly located near the other end of the spiritual yardstick. But the reality reflected in our local paper is true all over the world. When celebrities and leaders are asked whom they would most like to emulate, the answer is often Jesus, regardless of the person's faith background, or lack of one. Admiration for Jesus' sustained impact on our world is universal, and people want to know the man.

Like some of the people profiled in our paper, there are no doubt many readers of this book who don't share our spiritual perspective. You may have a radically different outlook on faith, hold no faith at all, or believe the jury's out regarding the existence of a Supreme Being. But we hold—and we're pretty sure you'll agree, no matter what you personally believe about him—that Jesus Christ was one of the most influential human beings who ever lived, and possibly the most influential.

His life split time into the era before and after His years on earth. Christianity, the faith His followers instituted, has inspired tremendous works of art, literature, and music. Wars have been waged in His name, swords drawn and guns fired. Some of these acts have strayed far from Christ's teaching of love and compassion, but others have been righteous movements for peace and justice: the movement to abolish slavery in the United States for one, and later a movement to grant equal civil rights to all citizens. Both had their roots in Christianity.

Historian Philip Schaff captures the ever-reaching influence of Jesus this way:

> Jesus of Nazareth, without money and arms, conquered more millions than Alexander, Caesar, Muhammad, and Napoleon: without science and learning, he shed more light on things human and divine than all the philosophers and scholars combined; without the eloquence of the school, he spoke words of life as were never spoken before nor since and produced effects that lie beyond the reach of orator or poet; without writing a single line, he has set more pens in motion and furnished themes for more sermons, orations, works of art,

learned volumes, and sweet songs of praise than the whole army of great men of ancient and modern times [in *Draper's Book of Quotations*, p. 352].

That's what I call clout—the kind that prompted these words by Baptist minister Dr. James Allan Francis: "All the armies that ever marched, and all the navies that ever were built, and all the parliaments that ever sat, and all the kings that ever reigned, put together, have not affected the life of man upon this earth as powerfully as has this one solitary life."

But what about Jesus' influence during His lifetime? Influence, as we have said, is the process of shaping people and outcomes. During the thirty-three years that He lived, Jesus was a model for expanding sustainable influence. He had regional influence in the world in which He lived, which mushroomed into worldwide influence after His death. His greatest influence during His life, of course, was on His immediate followers, many of whom later gave their lives as martyrs for the sake of their faith in Him. But His influence was not limited to the Twelve.

We see example after example of His influence during His interaction with people in ancient Palestine. Zacchaeus, the diminutive tax collector, was an outcast who had made himself rich by cheating others. But when Jesus saw him perched in a tree straining for a better look, He said, "Zacchaeus, come down immediately. I must stay at your house today" (Luke 19:5). Instantly, Zacchaeus was transformed by Christ's influence—His reaching out. He vowed to give half his possessions to the poor and to repay everyone he had cheated four times the amount he swindled.

Then there was Christ's encounter with the Samaritan woman at the well, recorded in John 4. The woman, an outcast because of her immoral lifestyle, came to draw water at a time when there wasn't likely to be anyone else around. Jesus, however, was there resting from His travels. During their conversation, Jesus revealed that He knew more about her life—and what was in her heart—than she would have thought possible. He also showed her love and compassion. The woman was amazed. She believed, and her life was transformed.

Jesus' interaction with an unnamed centurion and his sick servant was retold by two Gospel writers (Matthew 8:5–13, Luke 7:1–10).

The servant was getting worse by the hour, and a rumor began to spread that the miracle worker was nearby. The distraught centurion chased Jesus down and begged Him for help. Jesus responded by healing the servant without even setting foot in the house where the sick man lay—another demonstration of care and influence.

The life of Jesus reveals a strong picture of influence that's well worth taking a closer look. The Gospels give us a four-person point of view; by synthesizing these corroborating testimonies, we find five general statements about the influence of Jesus.

Jesus Embodied Influence

We couldn't find a clearer walking, talking example of Aristotle's Triangle if we tried. Jesus delivered a message that was meaningful, lived a life that was believable, and was aware of His audience and His environment at all times—usually to the point that His words and actions baffled His followers. They didn't understand the historical or societal context, but the Master did.

As we discussed in Chapter Four, the first chapter of John refers to Jesus as "the word made flesh." He was the living, breathing logos of God's message to humankind. In *The Master Plan of Evangelism,* Robert Coleman observed that Jesus "was his method." This truth is apparent not so much in what Jesus said or even what He did as it is in the quality of His being. He had an unusual connection to people of all kinds. At the end of His Sermon on the Mount, in which He turned Jewish teaching upside down with a radical new approach to interpersonal relationships and people's purpose for being on earth, the members of His audience "were amazed. He taught as one who had authority and not as teachers of the law" (Matthew 7:28–29). Jesus had something that the Jewish religious scholars did not. He was "the word made flesh," and He used His own divine humanity to influence the world. Theologians refer to this as *incarnation*: the divine becomes human.

Tom and I attended a meeting a few years ago in Skaneateles, New York. We were among a gathering of people who were harnessed by a common passion for the presence of faith in today's marketplace. Ken Blanchard hosted the meeting, along with Bob Buford, our friend and faithful field general on the front lines of the arena of faith in culture. Bob observed that our culture has moved from replication to proclamation to incarnation in how it receives truth. He made an arresting argument for the value of "a faith that is made flesh": we must embody the message we have proclaimed for two thousand years. We are, in effect, to be Christ to the world. Howard Hendricks said of unbelievers that "more is caught than taught."

The process of embodying our message, as modeled by Christ, is what we call *incarnational influence.* Paul sent Titus to the island of Crete with instructions to appoint elders who were models of Christian living so that their neighbors, by living with them and seeing them every day, could be influenced to live a holy life. More incarnational influence.

When Jesus first called the Twelve, He didn't hand them a four-inch-thick syllabus and a notebook to fill out. Rather, He called them "to be with him" (Mark 3:14). God's plan for redeeming the world was carried out through incarnation, and Christ's plan to influence a handful of followers was carried out through incarnation. Logging time with the Master was the plan two thousand years ago, and it's still the plan today.

The summer between my sophomore and junior years of college, a man of tremendous spiritual reputation was invited to speak at our church. Manley Beasley was his name, and influence was his game. I had been asked to help host this spiritual giant—take him to dinner, pick him up from the hotel, carry his bags, and so on. Late after dinner one evening, we were taking the elevator to his room when he said, "Steve, you know I am very ill and have required someone to travel with me these last few years. The fellow who has been my helper just called and informed me that he's leaving. Would you like to spend a year traveling and helping me?"

I accepted his invitation, and that short break in my formal education made as great an impact on my life as any of my bachelor's, master's, or doctoral studies. No college professor had a more powerful influence on me than did this professor of faith. What was the agenda? For me to hang with Manley Beasley. To spend time with him. Any assistance I gave him was secondary. He embodied his life message, which was a message of daring and radical faith. It was incarnational influence in full force.

Many of us have heard of Abraham Maslow's levels of learning and skill acquisition: unconscious incompetence, conscious incompetence, conscious competence, and unconscious competence. Manley had attained the highest level; he was unconsciously competent in matters of faith and influence. That's the way incarnational influence works. That's what Coleman meant when he said Jesus was his method.

What this says to us is that influence is more about being a certain kind of person than doing a certain set of things. Wherever we go, we are an influence merely because of who we are. Some people go to extreme measures to prop up their clout, or at least the appearance of it. But if clout is externally constructed, it will always be a little wobbly. The best kind of clout emanates from moral strength, which generates security that we feel and that is visible to others—security and significance built not on titles, money, or achievement. Rather, our internal strength is built on spiritual identity and an understanding that we were created with a purpose by a master designer, and we can have an intimate relationship with that same God. This settles me from the center of my being. Jesus influenced out of who He was, and we influence out of who we are.

JESUS PRACTICED INTENTIONAL INFLUENCE

It was not uncommon for Jesus to encounter a particular person or situation and immediately set about shaping that individual or circumstance. Many times He influenced sick people by making a disease or disability vanish. Other times He influenced people internally by opening their minds to a truth they had never known before. But His influence was never accidental.

There were four groups of people to whom Jesus customized His message for maximum impact. His radar was constantly sweeping these four groups, and He crafted His logos and read the relevant pathos to be intentional in His influence.

1. *Uninterested outsiders.* These were the masses, the multitudes. They were not necessarily looking for answers; they had no questions. Some were hostile, and some were indifferent. Some were marginally curious and wanted to see a sideshow—a miracle, perhaps. They were simply the crowds. As a general rule, it was fine for these uninterested outsiders to hang around. Jesus did not exclude them even if they did recognize or acknowledge Him. He didn't run off to hide with Peter,

James, and John. Instead He came to the synagogue, to the city gates, and to other places where crowds would gather. Jesus lived and walked among them, seeking out their traffic patterns. He was comfortable moving in and out of the multitudes.

2. *Interested observers.* At the appropriate time, however, Jesus pulled away from the crowds and focused on this smaller group: the scribes and Pharisees and others who had specific questions for Him. All of the parables are directed to interested observers—(people who raised their hands during question-and-answer time). This group wasn't necessarily looking for someone to commit to, but rather a role model— someone authentic and consistent who embodied the message. They were looking for someone to validate the claims of the gospel.

3. *Committed learners.* With similar intentionality, Jesus invited the twelve disciples to follow Him for a more intensive time of training. They heard the invitation to come and follow, and they said yes. Through their commitment, they moved from the role of observer to that of learner; they enrolled in school for an intense course about kingdom life. The New Testament word *disciple* can also be translated *learner.*

4. *Starving hearts.* These were Jesus' inner circle, among them Peter, James, and John. For a glimpse of Jesus' influence on these men, look at how they shaped the rest of the Bible—the books they wrote, the impact they had on the early church. Jesus had a sense of purpose and agenda with this intimate circle and with each of the four groups.

Another example of Jesus' intentional methodology was adaptation of His message on the basis of the societal position of the hearer. *Social down-and-outers* were hard-luck individuals at the end of every rope they had: physical, economic, mental, and spiritual. Jesus rarely approached these people with demands. Rather, He showed them compassion and acceptance. He didn't order them to make major sacrifices or lecture them about the wrong decisions they had made. He cut them slack and offered them grace.

On the other hand, *social up-and-outers* were in the upper class and aware there was something more to life than what they were experiencing. Christ challenged these people, with a tremendous amount of intentionality, to reach out for something beyond accomplishments and status. While Jesus showed these individuals compassion, He stretched them to an uncomfortable level of personal sacrifice, in part because they had more to begin with and therefore more to offer. To them, His logos was sprinkled with sharp, penetrating questions that forced them to grapple with deeper issues. Look at the encounter with the rich young ruler (Matthew 19:16–24), and watch Jesus in action.

Jesus' method for choosing, teaching, and influencing His disciples also clearly shows His intentionality. The Gospels spend much of their time recounting sessions in which Jesus deposited buckets dripping with kingdom information into the disciples' minds and hearts. But the lessons didn't end with the lectures. He also offered on-the-job training. In the true nature of influence, He gave them the ancient Palestinian equivalent of a briefcase, map, and rental car and sent them out on the road.

A mentor of Tom's and mine is a master in this regard. He has built his Fortune 100 company into a leader-growing incubator during the last thirty years. One of his secrets is to invest an extravagant amount of time and energy in the hiring process. When a prospective employee comes for an interview, our friend gets a feel for the person's work ethic, character, teachability, and believability. He even talks to the candidate about past failures. As the interviewee talks, our mentor friend listens with the skill of a veteran cardiologist attending to heart rhythms, aware of any irregularity. Once the new hire is on board, he gives the person the ball—in a big way. A new employee may be planning for an upcoming meeting, and our mentor will say, "Hey, Diane, I want you to give the presentation Friday." Or on a flight to visit the home office, he might ask his lieutenant to give the report to his peers and bosses. Every interaction is intentionally calculated to turn these people into successful leaders.

Influence doesn't just happen. It takes place with intentionality—the kind Jesus modeled.

Jesus Warned People *to* Take Influence Seriously

We see this principle flare up all over the New Testament. Two instances connected with Jesus bring it into focus. One was His constant badgering of the scribes and Pharisees. These professionally righteous people had become experts in doing religion but had lost the heart and soul of what religion was intended to be. They became self-focused and immune to their responsibility to be spiritual guides.

There's probably no better example of a group of people whose clout, over time, calcified into something useless at best, dangerous at worst. Jesus blasted these religious leaders repeatedly because they had become hypocritical in their influential positions and squandered their authority over the Jewish people. He did not have a kind word for their trivialization of influence.

Another strong warning about influence is found in Matthew 10, where Jesus brushes off His disciples' fussing and gathers a group of children around him. His message to the adults standing near is direct and chilling: whoever causes one of these little ones to stumble, watch out. It's better for you to tie a stone around your neck and jump into a lake than to face the consequences of your misguidance in the hereafter. Although Jesus was using children in this example, His message applies to anyone with spiritual influence over someone else, especially if that someone is trusting and vulnerable. We are to take our position of influence very, very seriously, whether as a coach with a Little League team, a parent with a child, or a teacher with a student. If I am in a position to influence a tender young learner, I must step forward with sobriety. I'm reminded of a scene from the movie *Spiderman,* in which the young Peter Parker leans over his dying uncle, who raised him. As his uncle takes his last breath, Peter hears his final words: "With great power comes great responsibility."

Impressionable minds and hearts surround us; we are to a great extent responsible for the outcomes of those lives. Our society could use a refresher to regain this sober understanding of accountability. We have lost any sense of uneasiness in this regard. We are too familiar, relaxed, and flippant about our clout. Politicians, pastors, police officers—all elements of our society—need a return to the awkward, unsettled awareness that others depend on us. Clout is more of a responsibility and a burden than a right. Jesus reminds us to take our leverage seriously.

JESUS HEIGHTENED *the* ROLE *of* INDIVIDUAL INFLUENCE *over* INSTITUTIONAL INFLUENCE

In his ministry, Jesus turned the world of Jewish tradition on its head. The religious teachers and leaders had immense sway over the people, but Jesus was less concerned with enforcing rules and regulations than

He was about the state of the individual's heart. Several times when the Jewish leaders saw things one way—healing a lame man on the Sabbath, judgment against a woman caught in adultery—Jesus saw them completely differently. He used the situation to change hearts rather than uphold an institutional code. In these cases, He sometimes informed people of their influence potential when they thought they had none.

Jesus was not advocating abandonment of all institutions, but He did challenge us to see beyond them to the level of the individual. We don't have to be part of an intricate hierarchy of structured leadership to exert influence.

Not too long ago, Tom and I were consulting with a family business going through a transition from first-generation to second-generation leadership. One of the founder's sons had attended college and returned to take over the company. This young gun straight out of grad school carried the family name, had the word *president* printed on his business cards, and was in the executive wing of the corporate office. He even parked in the special executive lot.

What this young man didn't possess was intrinsic natural influence. He'd never worked a day in the business and had nothing that would earn him respect: time-tested, battle-worn clout. His credibility wasn't bad, but it was empty.

Another young man of about the same age had worked his way up the organizational ladder, built relational collateral, and carried real clout in the business. The owner's son held positional power, granted by his family name and inheritance. The other employee could claim personal power he had earned. The new, young family leader needed to focus on building his ethos within the organization. Fortunately, he was quite teachable and possessed the quality of character that held him in training until the appropriate time for his coming out as the next leader of the company.

By its nature, positional power is external, and its trappings and symbols come and go with the position. The president of the United States flies on Air Force One until the day he leaves office. The CEO gives up her corner office (and, lately, perhaps a few more perks than in previous years) upon retirement. The coach can still call his players and the newspaper and talk about the game plan, but once he's gone, so is his positional clout.

Unlike positional influence, individual influence is earned. Moral authority serves as its energy source, and it flows from the inside out. The individual with personal influence knows her skills, knows what she was created to do, and conveys a sense of purpose. She experiences peace because her power relies on integrity, over which she has complete control, and it doesn't disappear when external circumstances change.

JESUS INTENDED HIS FOLLOWERS *to* ASSERT *a* HEALTHY INFLUENCE *on* THEIR SURROUNDINGS

What do you do with a lighted lamp? Jesus asked His disciples. Do you hide it under a basket? Ridiculous. What good is salt that's lost its taste? No good at all. "You are the salt of the earth," He said. "But if the salt loses its saltiness, how can it be made salty again? It is no longer good for anything, except to be thrown out and trampled by men. You are the light of the world. A city on a hill cannot be hidden. Neither do people light a lamp and put it under a bowl. Instead they put it on its stand, and it gives light to everyone in the house" (Matthew 5:13–15). Jesus' message is that we have a responsibility to illuminate and flavor the lives of other people. Embedded in this teaching are two of the most descriptive snapshots of influence, using universal and indispensable household commodities.

In Jesus' day, every home, however poor or rich, used salt and light. Come to think of it, everyone still uses them. But back then, salt, which was used for preserving as well as flavoring, was not refined as it is today. It contained bits of dirt, and the user had to pick out the salt from the mixture as needed and in the right proportion—too much would ruin rather than enhance, and too little was indiscernible. When all the salt was picked out of the mixture, the remaining dirt was thrown out. The salt had lost its flavor and its ability to preserve. In the same way, it was possible for a lamp to be shaded so much that it was equally useless.

Jesus was indirectly charging His followers to cultivate a sense of responsibility to influence appropriately and effectively. Unfortunately, zealots of every religious leaning have perverted this teaching. Jesus offered no element of "stilted optimism"—that is, misguided reassurance that culture would automatically spiral up and improve on its own. But when you stir positive, appropriate, effective agents of influence into the cultural mix, it can happen. Nor did Jesus advocate "fearful separation," removal from mainstream culture to a walled-off subculture. He did not disassociate Himself because He didn't want to taint His salt or waste His light. Salt must contact another substance to flavor or preserve; light must radiate if it is to illuminate.

The other evening, my family and I held a little meeting outside on the trampoline. The night was cool, the sky was wide, and the trampoline was stretched. (The teenage years for my kids and the middle-age years for their parents have really challenged this family tradition.) We unzipped our sleeping bags to create a giant family-size pallet, and we lay on our backs, side by side looking up at the pitch-black, moonless evening. The sky was crystal clear, punctuated by a million celestial spotlights. Our time together was a vivid reminder that when the night is the darkest, the light is the brightest. Our world feels dark at times, but God has placed individual, personal salt shakers and lighted candles all over the world to bring about positive influence, hope, and transformation.

God's communication strategy is usually to wrap truth around a person. That's exactly what we have in Jesus, the God-man, and that's exactly what God wants for us. Sheldon VanAuken, author of *A Severe Mercy*, said it well: "The best argument for Christianity is Christians. Their joy, their certainty, and their completeness. But the strongest argument against Christianity is also Christians. When they are somber and joyless, when they are self-righteous and smug and complacent, when they are narrow and repressive, then Christianity dies a thousand deaths."

In the movie *Finding Forrester*, the character played by Sean Connery was a lamp under a basket. A reclusive, eccentric writer, he stays in his apartment, refusing to interact with the rest of the world. Gradually, a gifted young student makes his way into Forrester's life, and a healthy, fruitful relationship develops. They influence each other for the better. People aren't meant to remain behind closed windows and locked doors. Jesus abandoned heaven to bring His influence to earth. That thirty-three-year visitation cast the most influential pebble into the pool of humanity that has ever been thrown.

• • •

KEY POINTS

- Jesus was a living, breathing example of the logos of God's message to humankind, and His plan to influence a handful of followers was incarnation. In short, Jesus embodied influence.

- Jesus practiced intentional influence; four groups of people were always on his radar screen:

  Uninterested outsiders

  Interested observers

  Committed learners

  Starving hearts

- Jesus always adapted His message to a person according to whether he or she was a social down-and-outer or a social up-and-outer.

- Jesus warned people to take influence seriously.

- Jesus was less concerned with enforcement of rules and regulations than He was about an individual's heart.

- Jesus heightened the role of individual influence over institutional influence.

- Individual influence, which is earned and has moral authority as its source of energy, flows from the inside out.

- Jesus intended His followers to assert a healthy influence on their surroundings.

- We have a responsibility to illuminate and flavor the lives of other people.

- God's communication strategy is usually to wrap truth around a person.

CHAPTER

8

Mentoring

Strategic Life Coaching

To know the road ahead . . . ask those coming back.

—Chinese proverb

OUTSIDE OF THE INFLUENCE DYNAMICS THAT take place within a family, mentoring may be the most direct, powerful, and long-lasting influence strategy that exists. We see examples of mentor-protégé relationships as early as the book of Genesis, but the concept as we know it today first surfaced as an actual character in Homer's *Odyssey*. The main character, Odysseus, holds his friend and steward, Mentor, in such high esteem that he entrusts his son's full education and care to the man before setting sail on his famous journey. The relationship between Mentor, a wise and trustworthy adviser, and Telemachus, an inexperienced young person, gave birth to the idea of mentorship, and the concept has remained relatively unchanged through the ages.

In the Roman period, Quintilian, a teacher of rhetoric and a contemporary of the Apostle Paul, wrote an educational curriculum called *Institutes of Oratory.* In it, he contended that a tutor, or mentor, ought to be of unimpeachable morals and wide knowledge; only the best of the best need apply. The educational system that Quintilian advocated was a years-long relationship in which the protégé was saturated with the learning and experience of the mentor. In addition to acquiring information, a student learned by imitating the life of his teacher. If what you imitate is flawed, Quintilian reasoned, then you will mirror those same defects.

From the Dark Ages to the Industrial Revolution, mentoring mainly took the form of apprenticeship. Serving as an apprentice was the primary way to prepare for almost any career. A prospective blacksmith or physician found someone to tutor him in that trade; no medical or other graduate schools existed until the 1700s. Apprenticeship lasted several years, and the apprentice usually lived with the mentor.

Today, the words *sponsor, coach, adviser,* and *intern* have joined the word *mentor* in filling the pages of business journals, magazines, and books. At first glance, these terms may seem to be a recent addition to a trendy vocabulary that also includes *total quality, reengineering,* and *team-based leadership,* or part of the shift to the "softer side of business." Or perhaps this emphasis is graying baby boomers' latest attempt to make a lasting contribution. Perhaps the new kids on the block are just quicker to ask for help and advice. Whatever the catalyst may be, the practice of mentoring and coaching is soaring. If you don't believe us, do a Google search and take a quick Internet cruise through some coaching and mentoring Websites.

A leading business magazine recently ran a cover story profile of a young up-and-coming entrepreneur who described a few informal encounters with his business hero as a mentoring relationship. But is that really mentoring, or is it water-cooler advice from a wise expert? How does it differ from other intentional transfers of influence and learning, such as parenting? Is mentoring a soft approach, or can it apply to the harder elements of life? Let's explore these and other related questions.

What Is Mentoring?

First, let's look at a glossary of terms related to mentoring. Even though they're often used interchangeably, these words vary slightly in meaning.

- Mentoring: a relationship with an intentional agenda to convey specific content and life wisdom from one individual to another.

- Advising: telling someone what to do.

- Coaching: an advising relationship in which an expert walks alongside another individual through a process or set of decisions.

- Counseling, consulting: a process in which someone with specific training and knowledge listens to another person and offers recommendations for steps that lead to improvement.

- Discipling: a mentoring relationship with the goal of training someone to be a follower of Jesus.

- Internship: the contemporary version of an apprenticeship, in which one is immersed in a real work environment to learn a service or skill.

- Protégé: someone whose welfare, training, or career is promoted by an influential person.

- Tutoring: private instruction that is customized around individual needs.

The type of mentorship described by the early Greeks and Romans, as well as in the Bible, does not happen by accident; nor do its benefits come quickly. It is relationally based, but it involves more than good friendship. Mentorship implies that of the two individuals in the relationship, one is primarily a teacher and one is primarily a student. It entails more than two people simply spending time together and sharing life experiences.

Over the last twenty years or so, Tom and I have been actively involved in mentoring and coaching. We call this element of our consulting practice *strategic life coaching*. Although mentoring and coaching differ in strict definition, they share many of the same goals, philosophies, and strategies. This chapter focuses on those overlapping elements, so we use the terms interchangeably.

Chris, the president of a large and growing not-for-profit organization, was one person with whom we shared such a relationship.

We had spent time with Chris on a number of occasions, liked him, and had come to understand his challenges fairly well. After a couple casual visits, we suggested that we explore a more defined working relationship.

It looked like this. We started by spending a few hours in what we call a white-board session—a fun, intense, confidential discussion of Chris's professional and personal worlds that involves lots of list making and diagramming. We then made a judgment about whether we could really help him and decided we could, and off we went. Our job was to walk alongside Chris for a predetermined period of time to work through a set of predetermined issues. (Later in this chapter, we look more closely at this process.)

First, let's explore in greater depth the definition of mentoring: a relationship with an intentional agenda to convey specific content and life wisdom from one individual to another.

A RELATIONSHIP

Open the pages of Scripture to study mentoring, and the first truth you encounter is that it involves a true, holistic relationship with no line between personal, professional, and spiritual. It is the kind that connected Moses to Joshua, Elijah to Elisha, Barnabas to Paul, and Paul to Timothy. All those pairings came about because one individual, under God's guidance, singled out another and initiated a significant relationship with mentorship as the primary purpose.

But the most complete record of mentoring in Scripture is the relationship between Jesus and His disciples. Jesus called a dozen men to follow Him and then stayed with them, more or less twenty-four/seven, for three years. The relationship between Jesus and the Twelve consisted of breakfasts on the beach (John 21:12–14), small-group huddles (Mark 9:2–13), moments of correction (Matthew 26:31–35), hazardous travel (Luke 8:22–25), and Q&A sessions (John 14:1–14). Jesus lived out who He was and what He taught before those He mentored, which authenticated His authority and message. The learning environment allowed the disciples to observe and experience Jesus, not just learn from His teaching; it's what we referred to in the last chapter as incarnational influence.

For example, in the Gospels we see Jesus continuously teaching the Twelve about prayer—a lesson here, a parable there. But at the same time He was explaining the truth of prayer, He was also modeling the reality of it. He invited the disciples to watch Him pray, and pray with Him. He encouraged them to pray about specific things. He freely and spontaneously broke out in prayer. Jesus was imparting the best kind of education.

Genuine mentoring and coaching involve an authentic personal relationship. This doesn't mean the mentor and protégé must become best friends, be together continuously, and share all vacations. It does mean, however, that the protégé has consistent access to the mentor. It also means that three relationally healthy elements must be in place.

First, there must be *chemistry.* Both parties must enjoy spending time together. In our coaching assignments, we try to plan activities to build this chemistry. An example for me is fishing. I've spent countless hours standing knee-deep or waist-deep in a river on a cool morning, a bright ball of warmth rising in the east, concentrating on fishing and strategic coaching—in that order. We fish a little, talk a little, think a little, then fish a little more. The pathos for strategic life coaching doesn't get any better for two guys who love to fish. I have friends who do the same thing during eighteen holes of golf on a sunny day at a spectacular course. If natural chemistry doesn't develop, the mentoring effort will roll into the ditch.

Second, there must be *available time.* I've seen perfect mentoring matches stall out because one person was simply too busy. A number of years ago, a young college student called me and asked me to mentor him. I struggled with the decision, vacillating on what my answer would be. I really liked this kid, and we seemed to have great chemistry, but I had no time. We were both sorry when I said no, but if I had agreed without the time to invest, we would have ended up much more frustrated and disappointed.

Third, there must be *similar interest* in the mentorship effort. If there's no appetite for the relationship, it won't last the full four quarters. A friend of ours has maintained for years that an available, motivated number two is always better than an unavailable or unmotivated number one. Although he uses that notion to pick business partners and clients, perhaps it has sound application in forging a mentoring relationship.

Every mentoring relationship is unique, but the knot that holds them all together is relationship. In some traditional ways of thinking, mentoring practices are related only to sponsoring someone's career or helping an individual with an isolated business issue. But true mentoring is much more holistic. It is a caring relationship that is based on mutual respect going beyond normal business boundaries, to extend into values, beliefs, and friendship. The intertwining of personal and professional worlds should be an unapologetic starting point in any mentoring initiative.

An Intentional Agenda

When Jesus called Peter off his fishing boat (Luke 5:1–11) and Matthew away from his calculator (Luke 5:27–28), He was inviting them to something more than a personal friendship. He was calling them to something more than a one-time experience with God. Jesus had three years in which to teach, persuade, shape, correct, forgive, rebuke, pray, and love these men into being capable ambassadors of God's salvation. He had just over a thousand days to inject Himself into their lives. He invited them to a full-time "influence lab" crammed with hands-on learning experience and practice drills.

Jesus called His disciples with a particular end in mind. With Peter and Andrew, He said, "Come, follow me, and I will make you fishers of men" (Matthew 4:19). Three years later, just before He ascended into heaven, Jesus offered a clarification of that agenda: "Go and make disciples of all nations, baptizing them in the name of the Father and of the Son and of the Holy Spirit, and teaching them to obey everything I have commanded you" (Matthew 28:19–20). Although the mentoring agenda became clearer to the disciples as the relationship progressed, Jesus knew exactly where the finish line was before the race began.

There are three continua involved in all mentoring:

1. Duration (short-term to long-term)
2. Structure (informal to formal)
3. Intentionality (inadvertent to deliberate)

Depending on goals and circumstances, any of these variables can change from case to case. Some coaching efforts last three months; others last two years. A course correction is often necessary to redefine the duration. Coaching is a lot like surgery; the surgeon knows how long a procedure normally lasts, but the time allotted can change dramatically once the surgery begins.

Highly structured mentoring is appropriate to bring a key employee on board or establish succession planning for a key leader. Less-structured coaching is suitable when someone needs general encouragement or accountability. In addition, we must remember that certain personality types need more structure than others do, while still others need a free flowing make-it-up-as-you-go approach to a coaching relationship.

It's important to recognize that not all mentoring relationships are equally intentional. Every mentoring relationship, once established, falls somewhere along each continuum. An intentional agenda also requires that we tailor the relationship to the personality, style, and needs of the protégé. Mentoring has no one-size-fits-all model. Generally, Tom and I focus our mentoring efforts on knowledge, skills, character, attitude, and vision. Sometimes we try to help develop all these attributes in parallel fashion, and sometimes we single out one or two for improvement and growth.

A mentor is someone who knows where the curriculum takes the protégé under his or her care. If the protégé wants to undertake any self-directed study, it's allowed only within tight parameters. Sometimes this singular focus can be mistaken for stubbornness or rigidity, but a gifted mentor has a clear agenda. When wrapped around a sense of fun, and with allowance for individual personality, an overriding goal does not come across as severe or inflexible.

Specific Content *and* Life Wisdom

During the early stages of any strategic life coaching assignment, we outline the objectives and seek agreement on the goals. Most of the time there is a specific issue or problem—we call it the alpha issue—serving as the catalyst for the engagement. It's amazing how similar the stories and issues are from case to case. A few years ago, the airline industry declared that all complaints related to air travel could actually be compiled into a very short list of "stock problems": lost luggage, rude agents, weather-related frustration, and so on. The same is true in strategic life coaching. The stock problems, or alpha issues, that we repeatedly face include first-season calling, second-season calling, balance between work and home or work and rest, generational transfer of a business, moral failure, financial concerns, and the like.

In our assignments, we are determined to place a barrel of information in the possession of the one being coached. The barrel has content regarding stewardship, calling, balance, work, and influence. A person's approach to these central issues shapes the outcome of the mentoring relationship. John Stuart Mill said, "Men are men before they are lawyers, or physicians, or merchants, or manufacturers; and if you make them capable and sensible men, they will make themselves capable and sensible lawyers and physicians."

Mentoring always includes teaching, but it is much more than the transfer of information or skill. A mentor has mastered both a specific body of knowledge and life wisdom and uses a unique combination of classroom learning and learning by doing. Mentoring should teach theory, but it should also prepare an individual for practical reality.

This is exactly what Jesus did with the disciples. The New Testament books of Matthew, Mark, Luke, and John are full of accounts in which Jesus taught the disciples, either alone or in a group. He often debriefed them after teaching a large crowd. In addition to formal teaching settings, He engaged in one-on-one dialogue (John 21:15–24), He moderated debate (Luke 9:46–50), He worked miracles (Matthew 4:23–25), and He took on the opposition (Mark 2:18–28). The disciples' on-the-job training also involved actually doing the work: going out in pairs to preach, cast out demons, and heal the sick (Mark 6:7–13). These instances, along with countless others recorded in the gospels, saturated the twelve protégés with the content and experience of Jesus' message.

The glue holding all the bytes of knowledge together is the wisdom that comes from exposure to the life of the mentor. In most formal teaching situations, class is over when the bell rings. The student has little exposure to how the teacher handles life as it happens. But a mentoring relationship includes experience in various contexts over time, so the mentor can demonstrate as well as explain. The student can probe deep, not just skate on the surface of an issue with a question that can be quickly answered and dismissed.

From One Individual *to* Another

Mentoring works best when there is an unambiguous understanding that the teaching and wisdom flow primarily in one direction at a time. One person is the adviser, and the other is the advisee. This reality flies in the face of a current cultural convention that supposes everyone has equally important information to share about all matters. It also assumes that a student is teachable and hungry to learn. Furthermore, it presupposes that the protégé is willing to be shaped in the image of the mentor.

Mentoring places a burden on both the mentor and the protégé. Mentors must understand that by agreeing to a mentoring process, they are obligating themselves to a relationship. Protégés must understand that they have a commitment to sit at the feet of the mentor. That phrase, *to sit at the feet of,* is figurative, but it does suggest an accurate picture of mentorship through the ages, including that of Jesus and the disciples. Does this mean the one being coached is weak and inferior? Not at all. Willingness to ask for help and to learn and grow is a sign of strength.

Flight instructors teach pilots how to fly. Coaches and trainers help athletes develop their physical potential. Physicians learn new medical techniques by reading about them, watching more experienced doctors perform them, discussing them, and then performing the techniques themselves. Parents and grandparents seek to shape their children and grandchildren into the kind of people they want them to become. In all these relationships, there's an understanding that the wisdom and knowledge flow in one direction.

Today's marketplace has changed drastically, and the role of mentoring has changed with it. About twenty years ago, the *Harvard Business Review* ran an article titled "Everyone Who Makes It Has a Mentor" (by Eliza Collins and Patricia Scott). In the article, three corporate executives discussed the place of mentoring in their career paths. At the time, it wasn't acceptable for mentoring to take place within a department, especially between boss and employee. Today, that philosophy has changed completely. It's common for a supervisor to mentor an employee, and the focus is probably no longer one-dimensional (simply on skills, attitude, or culture, for example). There's a more holistic approach to mentoring, with the relationship exploring all aspects of a person's life, not just the workplace.

The BENEFITS *of* MENTORING

These are some of the benefits of a healthy mentoring relationship in a business environment:

- Building loyalty and trust in the workplace.
- Creating a mechanism for growing leaders who will serve as a bridge to the future. Every organization is faced with the same situation: either grow the people they have or hire new ones. An important element of organizational change is a "leader-growing" environment.
- Retaining great people. Every year, new research is performed on what keeps people in their job. Money is a strong motivator, but it's not at the top of the list by itself. Opportunities to develop, grow, and make a meaningful contribution are consistently among the top three reasons people stay at a job.
- The chance to use hands-on, real-time training.
- The opportunity to open and improve relationship pathways.

The world of farming presents a metaphor for mentoring and coaching. A farmer nurtures a seed, from planting through harvesting. Mentoring is farming to grow people. Jesus often used agricultural metaphors, talking about sowers and seeds and referring to Himself as the vine and His disciples as branches. If you desire to grow and help others grow, get involved in mentorship. The harvest you reap may astound you. When it's all wrapped together, mentoring and coaching involve truth, accountability, and relationship poured from one life into another in some dosage—a proven formula for effective influence.

The FOUR PHASES *of* MENTORING

Sometimes people who want to get involved in mentoring ask what steps they should take. There are many effective models of mentoring, but one that we have used successfully for a long time involves four phases: identifying, connecting, evaluating, and affirming.

We begin by *identifying* the individual, issues, style, duration, structure, and expectations of the mentoring. The more due diligence during this phase, the better. We have experienced a number of coaching disappointments that could have been averted by better identifying on the front end.

Connecting requires spending time together to build relational chemistry. We work on projects with a protégé and engage in activities that enable us to log lots of time together. Sometimes it's helpful to widen the circle and connect within a larger group. When a person connects with peers, a terrific dynamic takes place. For ten years, I sat guys around a table facilitating a large men's group study. The larger group dynamic produced accountability and shared energy. Although we generally don't practice large-group coaching from start to finish, it can be helpful during the connecting phase. Plus, we love to introduce folks to other folks.

In the *evaluating* phase, we try to discern what's working and what's not working in the relationship: Are we making progress? Do we need to make adjustments? These evaluation checkpoints are important. It is important to periodically pull over and check the map.

Then we close the loop by *affirming*. Every effective mentor must develop proficiency in reinforcing and encouraging those he or she is trying to mold. Frankly, without those skills, would-be mentors are wasting their time—and that of their protégés.

This process may seem somewhat mechanical, but it doesn't need to be. Each mentor must work in a way that fits his or her style and personality. However, the elements of identifying, connecting, evaluating, and affirming generally show up in every successful mentoring relationship. Sometimes it's necessary to cycle back to previous steps; during the evaluating phase, you may realize you need to go back and reidentify the issues. If the focus is on the relationship and the goals and not on the structure, the mentorship will be free-flowing, unconstrained, and effective.

Take *a* Banana Over *a* Banyan Any Day

South Indian folklore offers a wonderful illustration of life coaching and mentoring. The banyan tree spreads its branches, drops air roots, develops secondary trunks, and blankets the land. A full-grown banyan can cover more than an acre. All sorts of animals, including humans, find shelter beneath its shady branches. But nothing grows under the dense foliage of a banyan tree. When the tree dies, the ground beneath lies barren and forsaken.

By contrast, the banana tree sprouts, and six months later small shoots appear around it. After eighteen months, the main trunk bears bananas that nourish all kinds of animals, including humans. Then the banana tree dies. But by this time, the offspring are full-grown, and in six months they bear fruit, and two years later they die. The cycle repeats itself over and over: new sprouts emerge every six months, grow, give birth to more sprouts, bear fruit, and die.

Mentoring is a banana-tree experience. It's a leader or a parent looking down the road and making a commitment to the next generation. It's not hard to come by; there are few people who would turn away an offer of healthy, beneficial mentoring. It doesn't take a genius or a perfectly successful life. It takes someone who's willing to carve out a portion of his or her resources and invest them for a purpose.

From Protégé *to* Mentor

I can trace the path of my life by the places I've lived, schools I've attended, cars I've driven, and streams I've fished. However, the most accurate track of my spiritual life is the presence of a series of mentors in my life. Two women serve as bookends—my mother on one end and my wife on the other—encompassing a series of relationships with godly men. I have picked up specific truths from each of the nine most influential people in my world, and each lesson was a product of that person's intentional, directed relationship with me.

During my reckless high school days, a basketball coach set his sights on this wiry kid from a single-parent home and said, I'm going to make an investment in you. He nurtured my self-image and gently (sometimes not-so-gently) nudged me toward the right, the good, and the pure.

Then, every Thursday afternoon during my freshman year of college, I met for two hours with a friend who taught me about the Scriptures. He stayed with me until I developed an appetite for truth and enough biblical understanding that I could feed myself.

While at another college, my favorite professor issued a standing Friday-night invitation: anyone up to the challenge could join him in a board game called Acquire. When added to his superb classroom teaching, this investment in our lives pushed the professor to the front of the influence line. Over cheese dip and Coke, I picked up some rock-solid life skills and character traits, in addition to a few shrewd board game maneuvers.

In an elevator in Memphis, Tennessee, I made the decision to sit out a year of my formal education and travel with Manley Beasley. He intentionally introduced me to the mystical side of following Jesus. Never again would I be satisfied with a textbook answer or a cold abstract argument for God.

Then, years later, a local business legend somehow took an interest in me. Over a ten-year period of time, he built a weekend MBA into my portfolio. What I know about certain aspects of business went from grade school to grad school, thanks to this mentor.

Get in the game of mentoring and coaching. You don't have to be a genius, or moving into early retirement. You don't have to be Mr. Personality or Ms. Life of the Party. You just have to be willing and available. Few things move the influence needle forward as mentoring does.

· · ·

Key Points

- Mentoring is a relationship with an intentional agenda to convey specific content and life wisdom from one individual to another. There are four elements of that definition: a relationship, an intentional agenda, specific content and life wisdom, and conveyance from one individual to another.

  A relationship: genuine mentoring and coaching involves an authentic personal relationship.

  An intentional agenda: Jesus called his disciples with a particular end in mind; He knew exactly where the finish line was before the race began. Three continua are involved in all mentoring:

  Duration: short-term to long-term

  Structure: informal to formal

  Intentionality: inadvertent to deliberate

  Specific content and life wisdom: mentoring always involves teaching, but the glue holding all the bytes of knowledge together is the wisdom that comes from exposure to the life of the mentor.

Conveyance from one individual to another: mentorship works when there is an unambiguous understanding that wisdom flows primarily in one direction: from adviser to advisee.

- When it's all wrapped together, mentoring and coaching involve truth, accountability, and relationship poured from one life into another in some dosage—a proven formula for effective influence.

- There are four phases in mentoring:

  Identifying the individual, issues, style, duration, structure, and expectations of the mentorship

  Spending time together to build relational chemistry

  Evaluating the process, to discern what is working and what needs to be amended

  Affirming and encouraging the person being mentored

- Mentoring doesn't take a genius or a picture-perfect successful life. It takes someone who's willing to carve out a portion of his or her resources and invest them for a purpose.

CHAPTER 9

Breaking the Genetic Code on Influence

Universal Models of Applying Influence

Give me a fulcrum on which to rest, and I will move the earth.

—Archimedes

UMANS HAVE BEEN FASCINATED WITH TOOLS for thousands of years. Archaeologists have found images of levers carved into five-thousand-year-old Egyptian sculptures. Jesus and Joseph couldn't run down to the corner hardware store, but the tools at their bench differed little in principle from the tools we use today. Carpenters in that day had long been using hammers, saws, chisels, files, drills, plumb lines, and rules. They knew then, as we know now, that success in life depends on having the right equipment.

For some guys, the best projects are those that require tools they don't possess, which gives them an excuse to drive to their hardware superstore and check out the latest prices and gadgets. Others love to dive into a job for which every necessary tool is lined up on the shelf in the garage.

A buddy of mine who lives in Nashville says that once a year, on a cool Saturday morning when the leaves are falling, a chainsaw spirit blows through his neighborhood. This unscheduled testosterone phenomenon begins when one neighbor wakes up (way too early for chainsaw noise), goes out to his garage, and fires up his saw. Then, as if by Harry Potter enchantment, all the men who live on the street roll out of bed, rub their eyes, grab their saws, and walk up and down the street clearing trees and underbrush for anyone who looks even half-interested. They work until midafternoon and then go sit on someone's back porch or by a toasty fireplace, drink a few beers, and talk about how rugged they are underneath their starched shirts.

One of the qualifications for this ritual is that you have your saw purchased, tuned up, and ready for action. The opportunity won't wait while you run to the store, buy a saw, then come back and join the games.

Sometimes the "need" for tools can be taken to an extreme. You probably know someone like our friend Bryan, who owns at least one of every tool made in the last fifty years. If we ever need a tool that we can't find at the Home Depot, Lowe's, or Sears, we know we can find it in Bryan's garage. For people like Bryan, owning the tool can be almost as satisfying as using it. Just knowing it's available gives him confidence in his workshop. The rest of us, however, don't think about tools until we're ready to use them.

When it comes to influence, we all have a few, if not all, the basic tools at our fingertips. They're sitting on the shelves of our life, waiting to be tuned up and activated. Here are six tools, some that you may use every day, others that are sitting on your shelf getting dusty and rusty, and still others that you don't currently own. The key to enhancing influence, just as in the workshop, is to master the tools at your disposal.

PERSONALITY and RELATIONSHIP

Perhaps the most natural and common way people influence others is through relationships—using the power of community and the strength of personality to make a positive impact on others.

Few things are more influential than personality. It's true in fifth grade, in high school, and in college, but it doesn't stop there. Every day we see adults charming, bullying, wheedling, and joking their way to greater influence, using some natural outgrowth of their personality to do so.

Sometimes we make the mistake of thinking only certain personality types can be effective, but this isn't the case. Shy people can have just as much influence as outgoing people, and a laid-back, take-it-as-it-comes type can make as much of an impact as someone driven by lists and schedules. We all have a personality type, and any personality type can be an effective influencer. A key to maximizing our personality strengths is to understand ourselves thoroughly, and to study how we interact best with people. When we know our natural strengths, we can capitalize on them. Gary Smalley and John Trent have identified four personalities, using the characteristics of certain animals:

1. Beaver: the task-oriented, busy, to-do list person who focuses on details
2. Lion: the type-A, alpha rooster with a take-charge personality
3. Otter: the fun-loving life of the party who enjoys being with others
4. Golden retriever: the steady, loyal, dependable helper who is always there

Theirs and other studies of personality and temperament are widely available and extremely helpful on the path to greater influence.

Brad has worked with us for some time. He's one of the most gifted people we've ever met at making friends and maintaining relationships. He reaches out to people easily and quickly establishes solid, lasting friendships. We had a talk with Brad the other day about this extraordinary gift. We asked him about his purpose in all these friendships and whether he'd ever thought of his list of friends as an asset over which he is a steward. A rich network of relationships is just as valuable as—if not more valuable—than—a seven-figure savings account or inheritance of a family business. Anyone with the ability to make and maintain significant relationships should handle them as an asset.

This issue brings to mind the parable of the steward and the talents:

. . . It will be like a man going on a journey, who called his servants and entrusted his property to them. To one he gave five talents of money, to another two talents, and to another one talent, each according to his ability. Then he went on his journey. The man who had received the five talents went at once and put his money to work and gained five more. So also, the one with the two talents gained two more. But the man who had received the one talent went off, dug a hole in the ground, and hid his master's money.

After a long time the master of those servants returned and settled accounts with them. The man who had received the five talents brought the other five. "Master," he said, "you have entrusted me with five talents. See, I have gained five more."

His master replied, "Well done, good and faithful servant. You have been faithful with a few things; I will put you in charge of many things. Come and share your master's happiness!"

The man with the two talents also came. "Master," he said, "you entrusted me with two talents; see, I have gained two more."

His master replied, "Well done, good and faithful servant. You have been faithful with a few things; I will put you in charge of many things. Come and share your master's happiness!"

Then the man who had received the one talent came. "Master," he said, "I knew that you were a hard man, harvesting where you had not scattered seed. So I was afraid and went out and hid your talent in the ground. See, here is what belongs to you."

His master replied, "You wicked, lazy servant. So you knew that I harvest where I have not sown and gather where I have not scattered seed? Well then, you should have put my money on deposit with the bankers, so that when I returned I would have received it back with interest.

"Take the talent from him and give it to the one who has ten talents. For everyone who has will be given more, and he will have an abundance. Whoever does not have, even what he has will be taken from him. And throw that worthless servant outside, into the darkness, where there will be weeping and gnashing of teeth" [Matthew 25:14–30].

If you're thinking this sounds as if friendship should have a hidden agenda, you're exactly right. Not an agenda for selfish gain—that's completely different, and we'll address it in Chapter Eleven. Our agenda in positive relationships is to help friends grow, improve, and move into a more vital relationship with God.

My wife and I sat down with one of our daughters the other day and had the kind of conversation many parents can identify with. It was about one of her friends. It seemed to us that this friend was influencing our daughter much more than our daughter was influencing her friend. This wasn't in itself the problem. The problem was that this girl had a bad reputation, came from a troubled family, and was a very needy child. We didn't object to our daughter spending time with this girl or other needy children, but we wanted her to use her friendships to give those kids what they need—a positive influence—just as we hope our daughter's healthy, solid friends will make a positive deposit in her life account as well.

The question we all need to ask ourselves is this: What are we doing to maximize our opportunity to make a positive influence with our relationship-building talents?

Knowledge *and* Ideas

As important a tool as relationship is, you don't have to have a personal relationship with someone to make a positive impact. Your knowledge and ideas can be a powerful tool, even with people you never meet.

Take this book, for example. Dozens of people worked to get it into your hands: writers, editors, proofreaders, a typesetter, a designer, prepress professionals who converted electronic images to film and then film to printing plates, printers who ran the press, workers who packed books in cartons and cartons on a truck, and a driver who drove the truck to a distribution center. Then someone at your bookstore ordered the book; another driver delivered the books from the warehouse to the store; someone unloaded the books from the truck and placed them on the shelf; and finally, someone sold you the book. You probably don't know any of these people, but their knowledge and ability to do their job well has influenced you (assuming, of course, that this book is influencing you).

Books and other printed media have been the most influential forms of communication in the world. That's why the founding fathers protected freedom of the press in the First Amendment. It's also why we should not rest until we have achieved 100 percent literacy in the United States. Every progressive society teaches its members how to read and write. Literacy lifts people to the level where they can reach the world of information, knowledge, and ideas.

A number of years ago, Tom and I were invited to Russia. We spent most of our time in St. Petersburg, meeting members of the political, academic, and business communities. Everywhere we looked, we saw the city's history in beautiful cathedrals and other impressive buildings.

At the same time, however, we were astonished by the lack of up-to-date information and ideas. We visited a toy manufacturer that covered several city blocks, but as we toured the facility we saw equipment that looked as if it dated from the 1950s. This company had not taken advantage of the technological advances we observed in other countries. At that time, just after the fall of Soviet Communism, many people in Russia weren't aware of what they didn't have. But with satellite communication and the ability to see the world from their living room, people are beginning to demand more information.

W. Edwards Deming is one of the greatest examples in this century of the power of an idea. A few years after the close of World War II, Deming, an American statistician, went to Japan to teach a course on statistical quality control. Japanese industrialists were immediately receptive to the idea of improving quality, and they embraced Deming's theory. The idea swept the country, and as Japanese industries began to rival American quality, Deming's theories became popular in the United States as well.

Time gives us a wider lens to view the Deming phenomenon in Japan and America. We can put it in the context of the Japanese work ethic and other factors that affected the rebuilding of the Japanese economy. We cannot deny, however, the large and lasting impact of a single idea on two of the largest economies in the world.

The writer Howard Hendricks said it well in *Values and Virtues*: "There is nothing in the world more powerful than an idea. No weapon can destroy it; no power can conquer it except the power of another idea."

Think about your knowledge, your ideas, and your life experience. What training have you received that could help people around you? What do you know that nobody else knows? Do you keep that information to yourself in an effort to solidify your power, or do you willingly share your information with others who can be positively influenced by it?

PLATFORM *and* TITLE

A doctor, pastor, coach, business executive, police officer, firefighter, mayor, actor, teacher, and parent all have a title or a platform from which to wield influence. Does somebody look up to you because of your title or position? Your responsibility, then, is to find a way to use this tool, your influence, with that person for good.

A while back, one of my daughters told me she needed to stop drinking sodas and drink more water.

"That's a good idea," I said. "What made you think of it?"

"My coach said it would help us stay in better condition," she replied.

Another scene happened a few days later. Sally, a friend of our family, told me her doctor recommended that she start exercising to lose weight. What did she do? Exactly what the doctor ordered. Why? Because he was her doctor.

Although I earned a doctorate, no one calls me Doctor except when they're teasing me. It's not on my business card. I don't even like to be introduced by it. Some would say I like the power of understatement; I've always liked that quality in others. However, our society just loves titles and labels.

In other countries and cultures, labels can be even more important. Former United Nations Ambassador Andrew Young took full advantage of this knowledge when he was mayor of Atlanta. "If a businessman dropped by on a moment's notice and wanted to come by and see the mayor, I would always drop what I was doing and spend five minutes with a potential investor in our city," he said. "It took me three minutes to hear what they were doing, and a minute or two to say thank you. Then we would stand and take a picture, and in less than 10 minutes it was over. One year, I met 152 different business leaders that way.

"Before they left, I would write my direct line to my desk and my home number on a card and give it to them personally. 'If you have any trouble, call me personally,' I would say. Not too many called, but, particularly with Japanese investors, where government has a lot of clout, for him to go back with a picture of the mayor and a business card with his home phone—that alone is enough to help a company make a decision to do business in Atlanta rather than in another city where the mayor wouldn't meet with them" (personal interview with author, August, 1998).

People defer to platform as well as title. Suppose your physician tells you that you need major surgery and asks you to seek a second opinion before making your decision. You won't go ask your Aunt Marge what to do. You'll ask another surgeon.

Such experts have tremendous influence and power, and they must take care to use it for good. What is your platform and title? Who follows your lead? What are you doing to make sure you lead people where they need to go?

Modeling *and* Lifestyle

I was standing around with other parents recently waiting for Julianne, my middle child, to finish volleyball practice. My friend Brad was waiting for his daughter as well. It was early in the season, and the coach had the girls running laps around the track, whipping them into shape.

All the girls had finished except one who appeared to be out of shape and not a good runner to begin with. She fell so far behind that she had an entire lap to go after the other girls finished and were bent over catching their breath. As the girl ran all alone around the track, I looked up and saw Brad's ninth-grade daughter, Sarah, jog back out and run the last lap with the other girl, cheering her on.

"Brad," I said, "that's really kind of your daughter."

"I don't know why she's doing that," he said. "I've never talked to her about that kind of thing."

"You don't have to," I said. "You and your wife model that kind of behavior every day, and Sarah just picked it up. That's your influence out there on the track."

In the previous chapter, we touched on the importance of modeling good behavior and lifestyle in the mentorship process. How we live influences others without our even realizing it. The example of our lives may be the most powerful tool in the toolbox.

Recently a giant-screen movie and well-publicized museum exhibits have reignited interest in the life of an obscure British explorer named Ernest Shackleton. I read his life story, and I'm on the list of those who are amazed by his feats of daring and survival. The quest he is most famous for could actually be considered a failure in strict terms of exploration: he didn't do what he set out to do, which was to traverse the continent of Antarctica. But it is an incredible tale of Shackleton's heroism and endurance in which men's lives were preserved in the most hostile and desolate terrain.

One day after setting sail from the continent of Antarctica to reach the intended starting point of their journey, Shackleton's ship became trapped in polar ice. It began to break apart under the pressure, and the crew was forced to leave it. They were able to make it back to land, but the chances of rescue were bleak. After five months of camping on the ice, Shackleton set out in an open lifeboat and sailed eight hundred miles to reach help. When he reached the island of South Georgia, he trekked across the mountains to get to the island's remote whaling station. There he organized a rescue effort and saved all the men he'd left behind.

There is little doubt that without the hope Shackleton offered his crew in his determination to live and preserve their lives, those men would have succumbed to the elements. Shackleton modeled a lifestyle of survival and hope in a situation that could easily have led to despair; his effort went down in history as one of the greatest expeditions of all time.

CHEERLEADING *and* AFFIRMING

Having someone believe in you can make all the difference, especially if it's someone you look up to. Several years ago, I was invited to speak to more than seventy thousand men at a Promise Keepers event at the

Silverdome in Detroit. My topic was "A Man in the Work World," and although I felt confident in my material I was certainly untested in this venue. Holding a microphone in front of a packed football stadium can be intimidating, to say the least.

Just before I walked out to take my turn, Bruce Wilkinson, author of *The Prayer of Jabez,* walked over to me and said, "Steve, I'll bet you have something very, very important and timely to share with all these guys today. I know you have prepared and I'm looking forward to hearing what you have to say."

Even old guys like me need a cheerleader. I immediately felt more relaxed and confident.

When I was a teenager working one of my first jobs, my employer said to me, "Steve, you might be one of the hardest workers I have ever seen." Not only did it boost me up at the time, I still try to live up to that compliment.

Honest affirmation and enthusiastic cheerleading are the easiest tools to pull out of the toolbox, and they can make all the difference in the performance of the people you influence. A friend of mine makes sure he gives as much energy to feed back to his leadership team after a presentation as he does in preparing them for the meeting. He shows them the way to improve, but he always identifies a couple things that they did outstandingly well. Ego biscuits taste great.

Find something to affirm in someone else, and you're on a wide freeway of influence with that person. The power of praise is huge. Robert Cialdini calls this the "principle of liking." People like people who like them. The challenge is to uncover real similarities and offer genuine praise, not empty flattery.

I recently met with the principal at the school one of my kids attends to register some concerns, but my approach was to affirm things the school was doing well. One of our earliest clients many years ago taught us this lesson. A board of directors had asked us to come in and evaluate their company. Its growth was rocketing, and the company had never had an outside assessment. The board wanted us to identify areas of growth and development, so we did. But in our report we mentioned only the elements that could improve and develop. By the time the document was passed from the board to the executives and back, we had been labeled as negative. We had observed many strengths worth celebrating, and we talked about them freely, but we didn't put them in the report. From that day until now, we always register successes along with areas that need improvement.

I have tried to apply this principle to my life of parenting, relating to my spouse, struggling with an airline over a flight, coaching my kids in sports, and coaching executives regularly.

You might want to ask someone close to you which comes out of your mouth first: the positive or the negative. As we were so many years ago, you might be surprised by the answer.

HUMAN GOODWILL *and* BENEVOLENCE

A man stood at the corner of the busiest intersection in our town during the Christmas holidays, holding a sign that read, "Will work for food." My kids were with me in the car as I drove past him going into the mall and again coming out. A block down the street, however, I changed my mind. I stopped, turned around, and gave him some money. I didn't have a job for him.

"What if he doesn't use the money for food?" one of the children asked.

"That's God's problem, not mine," I said. "My responsibility is to share."

I wish I could say I make all the right decisions when it comes to sharing. I'm not even sure that one was right, but it was the best I could do with limited information. My hope is that for one moment, that man knew that at least one family in the world cared about his well-being.

Goodwill and benevolence are strong tools in distributing influence, although the results often seem more like a mystery than an intended consequence. Jesus told the parable of the good Samaritan to reinforce the principle of giving:

A man was going down from Jerusalem to Jericho, when he fell into the hands of robbers. They stripped him of his clothes, beat him, and went away, leaving him half dead. A priest happened to be going down the same road, and when he saw the man, he passed by on the other side. So too, a Levite, when he came to the place and saw him, passed by on the other side. But a Samaritan, as he traveled, came where the man was; and when he saw him, he took pity on him. He went to him and bandaged his wounds, pouring on oil and wine. Then he put the man on his own donkey, took him to an inn, and took care of him. The next day he took out two silver coins and gave them to the innkeeper. "Look after him," he said, "and when I return, I will reimburse you for any extra expense you may have." (Luke 10:30–37)

First, we see that the Samaritan had a heart that cared. He felt pity and was moved by someone else's plight. If you don't have a caring heart, then fall on your knees and pray that God will give you one. He will.

The Samaritan also had eyes that spotted someone else's need. To be compassionate, we must train our eyes. It's like the *Where's Waldo?* books so popular with children. The first few pages you look at are busy with ink and activity, and you think you'll never find Waldo. But after a while, your eyes are trained and Waldo practically jumps off the page at you.

Third, the Samaritan had hands and feet that took the initiative. He wasn't just paying back a favor. Sometimes it takes discipline to seek an opportunity to serve others.

Finally, the Samaritan was flexible. This man wasn't wandering around the mountains looking for stranded, beat-up travelers. He had his own agenda, his own to-do list. But he made time in his schedule when an opportunity to serve another arose. We shouldn't schedule our time so tightly that we can't respond to an opportunity for goodwill.

"Ask Me About My Miracle"

The same woman has been giving me the same haircut for seventeen years. Once a month I go into her shop, and she takes a little off the top and shapes up the back and sides, all the while engaging me in the comings and goings of northwest Arkansas. Like anyone who has been cutting hair for any length of time, she trades in insider information, and I enjoy learning what's going on.

About a year ago I went in, plopped down in the chair, and saw right away that she was discouraged. I asked what was bothering her, and she unfolded her story. Her daughter had just been in an accident with her granddaughter in the car. The little girl had been released from intensive care, but she was paralyzed from the neck down. Because of other circumstances in the mother's life, the girl was being taken into custody by the state of Arkansas.

My friend, the girl's grandmother, offered to take the child into her home. This fifty-two-year-old woman and her husband were beginning their second go-around rearing children. The demands were great; they would have been so even without the girl's paralysis.

The other day, though, I walked in for my monthly trim and she said, "We had a miracle last night! Ask me about my miracle."

"Tell me about your miracle."

"My granddaughter pulled herself out of bed with the help of a bar. I'm so thrilled!"

I listened as she described this life-changing event. "What a wonderful return on the investment of your influence," I told her. This woman was spreading human goodwill. She was modeling. She was being a cheerleader.

With her influence toolbox, my friend is changing the world for a seven-year-old girl. Her tools were clean, oiled, and ready for the opportunity. I hope mine are in the same condition. Are yours?

This learned I from the shadow of a tree,
that to and fro did sway against a wall,
our shadow selves, our influence, may fall
where we can never be.

Anonymous

• • •

KEY POINTS

- When it comes to influence, everyone has a few (if not all) of the basic tools he needs, already at his fingertips.
- Personality and relationship are perhaps the most natural and common ways people influence others.
- Knowledge and ideas are a powerful way to influence people, including those we have never met.

- Platform and title give us a position from which positive influence on others can be exercised.

- Modeling and lifestyle give me an opportunity to live out in front of folks the kind of life I am recommending to them.

- Cheerleading and affirming are two of the easiest tools to pull out of the mentoring toolbox. They can make all the difference in the performance and mind-set of those over whom I have influence.

- Human goodwill and benevolence figure strongly in the distribution of influence, although the results are often in the category of mystery rather than intended consequence.

- Jesus' parable of the Good Samaritan gives us a step-by-step guide for anyone wanting to improve her giving.

Influence Has an Org Chart

Understanding the Four Spheres of Influence

When a man is wrapped up in himself,
he makes a pretty small package.

—John Ruskin

THE MOST UNUSUAL ORGANIZATION CHART I
have ever seen was presented some years back during a strategic
planning meeting Tom and I were facilitating for a family-owned and
family-operated company in the Midwest. All the family was present
and all the executives accounted for as the annual meeting kicked off.
Our role was to help steer the process.

Like many successful second-generation businesses, this small
company was poised to step out of its regional arena to become a national force in its industry. The vice president of human resources, a
bright, free-thinking young man, had been assigned the task of creating an organization chart that would catapult the company into its
prominent new position.

The company had created a culture of creativity and affirmation,
and the HR director played a major role in maintaining that environment. For example, the annual Christmas celebration he organized

was so exciting that some in the company wondered if their HR director had Broadway experience in an unknown former life. This fellow—we'll call him Dave—supported an environment where every success was affirmed, often dramatically.

That same spirit found its way into his presentation of the proposed new org chart, which he rolled out during this annual meeting. And roll it out he did. The presentation was a Disney-style experience complete with all three of Aristotle's necessary elements of persuasion. But as the pathos cleared off and it came time to focus on the logos, the message, the room rumbled.

Dave had created a huge poster with a pie chart as its centerpiece. Nothing terribly unusual there, but he had also drawn circles everywhere. They overlapped. They were different sizes. Some were connected. Some stood alone. There were also dotted lines, thick bold lines, thin weaving lines, and in some places no lines at all to show reporting relationships.

The executive team approached the chart as if they were in a modern art gallery. They walked up close. They turned their heads. They slowly backed up, tilting their heads first in one direction, then the other. The masterpiece before them looked like an amalgamation of American impressionism, art deco, and Western corporate design theory. The chart wasn't approved, but it created some fantastic dialogue that pushed this company toward even greater innovation as it grew. (In hindsight, perhaps that was Dave's single agenda: he was acting as a creative entertainer trying to shock his audience into seeing things differently.)

A company creates an org chart to give people on the inside and the outside a clear blueprint of roles and responsibilities. The chart shows who reports to whom and how people relate to each other and the rest of the organization; it is a road map for strategy and relationships. In the same way, an individual can create a personal organization chart for structural guidance in channeling influence. My chart would show how individuals and groups in my world relate to one another and to me. By analyzing the many relational networks surrounding us, we can customize our approach to influence. Then we can apply the tools we discussed in Chapter Nine with even greater impact.

FIELD-TESTED *in the* NORTHEAST

A few years ago, I visited a college friend who had moved from the Mississippi Delta to Pittsburgh, Pennsylvania, to pastor a church. He had been in Pittsburgh for a few years, and his ministry was thriving. Over dinner I asked Dan how in the world a barefoot boy from Mississippi could be so effective with the Yankees in the Northeast. He unfolded his blueprint and gave me a peek at his construction plan. He had an org chart for influence that was guiding his structure and strategy.

Dan had attended a conference and heard Tom Wolf, who was then a professor at Golden Gate Theological Seminary in San Francisco, speak about effective ministry in urban settings. Wolf shared example after example of effective ministry models he had observed around the world. Then he shared a common insight built from a single Greek word. Wolf unpacked its meaning and implication, and with that word he transformed my friend Dan and his approach to church leadership.

Wolf's focus was the word *oikos* (pronounced "EEH-kos"), which appears a number of times in the Bible and in its simplest definition means *house*. He went on to say that in modern Western culture, we think of that word as describing a physical building, or at most a household or family. However, in the Mediterranean world in which the New Testament was written, the word *oikos* actually meant *network* or *sphere*.

The word is used in Acts 20:20, where Paul says, "You know that I have not hesitated to preach anything that would be helpful to you but have taught you publicly and from house to house" (oikos to oikos). This doesn't mean, as many have assumed, that Paul was advocating a door-to-door, cold-call approach to evangelism. It means he was teaching and applying his influence from network to network, sphere to sphere, oikos to oikos.

Oikos is used in Acts 10 in the story of Cornelius. When Cornelius received a vision from God's angel, he invited Peter not just into his house, but into his world—to meet his family, his close friends, and his colleagues from the roman Regiment. The word shows up in John 4 when Jesus talks to the Samaritan woman. After their encounter, she returned to her city and persuaded many of her friends and associates—people in her sphere of influence—to believe in Him as well.

It's also used in Acts 16, which gives the account of Lydia's conversion and her invitation to the apostles to come to her home. Upon receiving Christ's message, these people didn't go to the mall and try to convert strangers. Each one returned to his or her network—to his or her oikos—and exerted influence there.

According to Tom Wolf, we all live within a fourfold highway system that constitutes a great organization chart for influence:

1. Biological, which includes our families
2. Geographical, which involves people whose path we cross in our "traffic patterns"—at the store or restaurant we frequent, the places we visit regularly
3. Vocational, which involves colleagues at our workplace
4. Volitional, which includes people we know through a hobby or outside interest

The message is clear. On the basis of the teachings of Aristotle and Jesus, and our observation of our own lives and routines, we can say that the most natural arena for influence is in our daily relational encounters. This is where our ethos makes an impact; this is where we're familiar with the elements of pathos; this is where we can adjust the logos. And that's our individual influence org chart.

Biological Oikos

Each of us has a family tree—some are more stately than others. There are perfectly groomed trees, which might be supporting a blockbuster family of husband, wife, three children, five grandchildren, all grandparents alive and healthy, and all living within a few blocks of each other. If you saw the 2002 hit movie *My Big Fat Greek Wedding*, you laughed at the consequences of uniting two extremely different family trees. The bride's Greek family tree, with its dozens of cousins and aunts and uncles, looked like a gigantic olive tree with its strong limbs twisting in and around each other. The groom, on the other hand, had only his father and mother—a frail, spindly family tree. But just like

Charlie Brown's Christmas tree, any family tree can stand stately and strong with enough love and positive influence.

Within the biological oikos, we see four basic relationships: parent to child, child to child, child to parent, and family to family. Our influence in these connections is determined by our application of the tools of personality and relationship, knowledge and ideas, platform and title, modeling and lifestyle, cheerleading and affirming, and goodwill and benevolence.

Parents Influencing Kids

The most natural, built-in mechanism for influence is the parenting process. However, the weight and pace of parenting often sucks the wind from our sails, and we lose the energy for intentional influence. No clout is simultaneously so easy and difficult to wield as that of a parent. Parents influence their children by accepting them, by helping them be successful, by helping them accept themselves, by protecting them, and by raising them to be morally responsible and self-reliant.

Two objectives rise to the top of the list of ways parents should influence their kids. First, they must transfer the claims of their faith. When children leave home, they need the roots of a genuine, vital, personal life of faith. Second, children must have a healthy self-image, from the inside out. When they look in the mirror, children should like themselves and be comfortable with the person God created them to be. With that perspective comes self-reliance. Those two goals are the parenting assignment at its core for all of us.

Completing the assignment successfully requires that parents alter their game plan and select the proper tools to match the situation, just as a good coach changes her strategy from game to game. We have to change because our children need to have us relate differently to them through various stages of their development. Growth from toddler to preschool to elementary school happens in the blink of an eye, but the needs of a six-year-old bear little resemblance to those of her two-year-old sister. For many parents, the middle school years are a fight for survival; high school is the final preparation for independence. Of course, our children will forever be our children, and our opportunities for influence continue through college and beyond. The point is that our methods must change. In the early years, platform and title— "I'm the mother and I said so"—may be our strongest tool. Later, however, personality and relationship are the key to influencing teenagers and young adults.

Additionally, we should adapt our style to the needs of each child. My wife and I have friends in Utah with two sons. They are an athletic, outdoors-oriented family that enjoys skiing, hiking, biking, anything that gets them outside together—except for the older son, Brad. While the rest of the family goes snowshoeing, Brad reads by the fire or cruises Internet discount shops. In contrast to his fresh-faced, clean-cut family, his hair has been every color of the rainbow and his fashion taste runs to the other side of the street. He's wired totally differently from the other family members. Early on, his parents recognized this bent in Brad and planned activities around his interests (museum visits, concerts, and so on). Then they took advantage of those opportunities to influence their son positively. Even though Brad looks different and prefers books to bikes, he shares his sibling's personal faith, and he is as confident in who he is as the rest of the family are. The family is a model for accepting, loving, and releasing people to be themselves.

All parents should regularly ask themselves—independently, together, or both—if they are influencing their children actively and correctly. Dads particularly need to make sure they don't miss out on opportunities. Influence is not just a mom's job.

Kids Influencing Kids

Siblings argue and fight, but they also shape one another—in some cases, more than parents do. I often ask my kids where they learned something, and they repeatedly say "from my brother" (or sister). Although much sibling-to-sibling influence is the teaching of skills or passing along of knowledge, brothers and sisters also greatly affect character. Sometimes moral courage can be transmitted between siblings better and with more ease than from parents to children. An older sister who says no to peer pressure can make a much more significant impact on her sibling than can a lecture from Mom or Dad.

The whole family needs to buy into the total-systems approach to positive influence. Older siblings particularly should understand the effect of their actions and words on their younger brothers and sisters, and that they bear a responsibility in that regard. At the same time, parents should take care not to make "little parents" of the older siblings. A child who thinks he or she is in charge of everyone in the family can create more resentment than positive influence.

Kids Influencing Parents

Children have tremendous influence with their parents, and parents can learn much from them. The process begins when we engage ourselves with our children and see the world through their eyes. Jesus said, "I tell you the truth, unless you change and become like little children, you will never enter the kingdom of heaven" (Matthew 18:3).

Let your young children's enthusiasm for life be contagious. Throw yourself headlong into life the way they do. Trust the way they trust you. Your child will leap from dangerous heights if you are standing there to catch him, because he trusts you. Do you live a life worthy of that trust? Few weeks go by that engaged parents don't think about the lessons they learn from their children.

Family Influencing Family

There's a real need for interfamily influence in our society. Two-income families, single-parent families, long distances between grandparents and grandchildren, job transfers, and other factors leave too many children lacking in stable, long-term adult role models.

How many times in recent years have you heard about grandparents rearing a second family because their own children were incapable parents? The good news is that there are grandparents available and willing to make that incredible commitment.

When the opportunity arises within and beyond our family, we should make ourselves available to assist in bringing up the next generation. My friend Ted and his son have befriended Mark, a fellow third grader, who has become like a member of their family. Mark's own father died, and the empty space in his life was obvious. Ted and his son invite Mark to join them at sporting events, and Ted has chosen Mark to play on recreation sports teams that he coaches. I know how important this kind of outreach can be because I did not have a father for much of my growing-up years. Certain men stepped in to help fill that gap.

Jim the Boy, a beautiful little novel by Tony Earley, tells the story of a boy growing up in the 1930s whose father died a week before he was born. His mother's three brothers live within walking distance of the farm, and at one point in the book they persuade Jim's mother to listen to the marriage proposal of another man. Jim needs a father, they insist. But when Jim, who is ten years old, hears of the plan, he asks his uncles, "Why do I need a daddy when I have the three of you?"

VOCATIONAL OIKOS

A friend of mine who worked for a small company was interviewing a potential new employee, who had already interviewed with the owner of the company. As they were talking, the interviewee mentioned to my friend, "Your boss described you as 'the conscience of the company.'" My friend was taken aback by the comment. He had no idea he held that kind of influence with the ownership. He later told me, "From then on, it put a burden on me to conduct myself in a manner appropriate for a 'conscience.'"

How can you be a positive influence at your workplace? How can you be your company's conscience? A good role model is Joseph. He had every reason to be bitter and resentful; his brothers had sold him into slavery. But there is no record of any complaints from Joseph. Eventually, an officer of the Egyptian Pharaoh brought him to work in his house. Joseph did his job so well and brought his influence to bear so effectively that he was remembered at promotion time. In fact, Potiphar left all that he had in Joseph's charge. Then Potiphar's wife lied, accusing Joseph of assaulting her, and Potiphar had him thrown into prison. Again, Joseph might have turned bitter, but instead he became a model prisoner and was made captain of the guard.

So even if you're facing the worst and you feel like a slave or a prisoner in your work environment, if you perform like Joseph, without complaint or bitterness, people will notice and you will influence them positively.

Tom and I wrote a set of four little books a number of years ago. We had been asked to speak at a national men's conference on the topic of work and were asked, "What should every person of faith look like at work?" Naturally, a number of qualifiers affect that answer, but we researched the question, taught on the subject, and then wrote a series of booklets on the idea that every man and woman of faith should have at least four things, regardless of the work situation:

1. Serving: the art of focusing on someone else's interests instead of one's own

2. Skill: understanding something completely and transforming that knowledge into creation of wonder and excellence

3. Character: the sum of one's behaviors, consistently arranged across the spectrum of one's life

4. Calling: God's personal invitation to work on His agenda, using the talents one has been given in ways that are eternally significant

With a commitment to these four goals, anyone can exert significant influence within his or her vocational oikos.

GEOGRAPHICAL OIKOS

If a satellite camera traces our comings and goings, we will probably be surprised by how often we cover the same ground, visiting the same stores, restaurants, and recreational facilities—and seeing the same people. This is our geographical oikos. Week in, week out, we see many of the same people again and again. How do we influence them? Are we using the tools of influence discussed in Chapter Nine to make a positive impact?

On many Sundays, I take my family to lunch at one of our three or four favorite restaurants, and the people at each place know us well. One Sunday, a couple we had known for years but never run into while eating out came into the restaurant; you would have thought they owned the place. The hostess knew them, the waitresses knew them, half the customers knew them, even the cook spoke to them.

We chatted with them as they passed our table, and I asked, "How is it that everybody here knows you? We've never seen you eating in here." They explained that they came often during the week, but they usually didn't eat there on Sundays.

Two things were happening here: our family was making its impression in this particular restaurant on Sundays, while our friends had been making their impression on other days during the week. But the restaurant staff had an opportunity to make an impression on both families, and many more who came through its doors.

Sometimes we exert our greatest influence by not showing up at all. The fast-food restaurant chain Chick-fil-A, for example, closes on Sunday, which is the most profitable day of the week for many establishments. Every week the company receives letters of thanks from employees and customers for that strong statement of principle.

What statement are you making within your geographical oikos?

VOLITIONAL OIKOS

I heard a speaker tell a story about a golfer named Frank who attended his church. Every Saturday morning for twenty years, Frank teed off with the same foursome. Then one Saturday, one of the other golfers, Robert, said he was going to miss their game for a couple of weeks because he was helping some new friends build a Habitat for Humanity house on Saturdays.

"How did you get involved in that?" Frank asked.

"I visited a church last Sunday," Robert said. "They're building it, and they invited me to help."

"What church is that?" Frank asked.

He told him, and Frank said, "Hey, that's my church. You visited my church last Sunday?"

Frank's partners all looked at him. "You go to church?" one of them asked.

When Frank confessed this story to his minister, he had tears in his eyes. In two decades of playing golf with the same three men every Saturday morning, he had never once mentioned that he went to church on Sundays. He had so carefully categorized the various areas of his life that he never let conversation about one area overlap into another—particularly his spiritual life. He didn't want to come across as preachy.

Frank's golfing partners decided it would be a great idea for all four of them to take a couple of weeks off from golf to help build the Habitat house, and after two Saturdays working together to serve others they became true friends, not just acquaintances, after all those years.

It all started with one man willing to make a choice—and willing to talk about it.

Our volitional oikos, the places we go and people with whom we spend our discretionary time, affords a wonderful opportunity for influence. People we run into regularly at the gym or at our children's soccer games respond positively when we do or say the right thing. We don't have to announce our good deeds on the town square, but neither should we hide our light under a basket.

WHERE IT ALL STARTS

You may be saying, "I understand the spheres, but I'm not sure what I'm bringing to the people in my spheres. What am I am influencing them *with*?" The answer is simple: *goodness.*

Many Christians may object and say that only the pure, unencumbered gospel is worth bothering about when it comes to influencing others. However, in Matthew 5, when Jesus was teaching His followers about salt and light, He ended with a curious summary. He said we should display such attractive good works that everyone else can tell we are wired differently. Our goodness falls well below the mark in meriting our salvation, but Scripture is replete with admonition to do good works for the sake of influencing others, and that is a high mark.

A successful entrepreneur in Chicago once explained how important that mark is in his hiring policy. "I look for good people who see the good and practice the good," Joe said. "Find them, and you have a gem. I can mold them to do the job I need for them to do. But if they are not good people to begin with, we start a downward spiral that ends in failure."

One of the most dramatic stories of influence for the church comes from a little paperback book that recounts the story of Patrick, born the son of a culturally Roman, Celtic priest in about 385 A.D., captured by Irish raiders at the age of sixteen, and sold into slavery. For six years, according to Patrick's autobiography, he tended his master's sheep. Author George Hunter, in his book *The Celtic Way of Evangelism,* analyzes the change Patrick experienced and his unique style of influence, which converted virtually all of Ireland from paganism to Christianity.

Three things happened to Patrick, Hunter writes, while he was watching his master's sheep. He experienced natural revelation, praying one hundred times daily and even more at night. He spent an enormous amount of time with the Celtic people, learning the language and their customs. He experienced an overwhelming, God-inspired love for his captors.

He escaped slavery and went back to England, but he later returned to Ireland, which was then populated by barbarian druids, intent upon sharing his faith with his former captors. He could have followed the Roman model of evangelism—ministry, conversion, and friendship—to attempt to convert the Irish. But Patrick didn't believe such a system would influence these people. So he reversed the order and sought friendship first, then conversion to a belief in Christ, followed by ministry.

He built relationships—real friendships with the people within his spheres of influence. Then he told them interesting stories about his faith, which they enjoyed hearing and which allowed them to warm up to the idea and person of Christ.

Sixteen hundred years later, Patrick's model of influence remains the most effective one for making a lasting influence on other people: relationship first. The depth of our influence in each of our four oikos spheres depends on our desire and commitment to build relationships.

• • •

KEY POINTS

- Analyzing the many relational networks around us allows us to customize our approach to influence.

- Our sphere of influence, or oikos, includes four elements from which our organization chart of influence can be formed:

  Biological: immediate family and extended family

  Geographical: people we run into through the traffic patterns of places we frequent, including restaurants, stores, schools, soccer games, and so on

Vocational: colleagues and associates, at and through work

Volitional: folks we know through outside interests and hobbies

- Biological oikos, which is likely the most natural, built-in mechanism for influence, includes parent-to-child, child-to-child, child-to-parent, and family-to-family relationships.

- Vocational oikos gives us the opportunity and permission to build influence in the place where we will spend between 90,000 and 130,000 hours of our life: at work.

- Every person of faith ought to evidence through his or her work, at the least, four elements: serving, skill, character, and calling.

- Geographical oikos asks us to take stock of the people we run into regularly in the course of our daily routine. We see many of the same people over and again. How are we influencing them?

- Volitional oikos involves the traffic patterns we travel in our discretionary time: playing golf, going to a movie, spending a weekend camping, and so forth.

- Evidencing goodness is the beginning point for all sphere-of-influence options.

When Influence Becomes Influenza

Influence Gone Bad

Whether the knife falls on the melon or
the melon falls on the knife, the melon suffers.

—African proverb

A LIFELONG READER, I HAVE BEEN ADDICTED to newspapers, magazines, and books for twenty-five years. Throughout those two and a half decades, I've seen rags-to-riches and success-to-failure stories hit the front page week after week, each one generating its own brand of speculation, gossip, and media feeding frenzy.

However, no modern account can rival the drama and heartbreak of a story that happened more than three thousand years ago. It's the tale of an early franchise player named Saul. He was born with a silver spoon in his mouth, into a very wealthy family. Taller and stronger than anyone else, he was physically striking—he turned heads then and would do so today. His personality was winsome and commanding. He was brave beyond comparison. He was a patriot who inspired nationalism and hope the way a New York firefighter would at a Sunday church service or Monday company meeting in the Midwest. With the blessing of God and the support of the people, he was anointed as the first king of the nation of Israel.

He had a great beginning. Such promise. But as Saul's story makes painfully clear, a strong start doesn't necessarily translate into dramatic, long-term influence.

Saul finished tragically. His end was not just bad, mind you—it was a tragedy of Shakespearean proportions, the kind that makes us shake at the core even thousands of years later. He died a coward, full of paranoia, void of faith, committing suicide. Why? How? What happened? The man who at the start stood head and shoulders above the rest, literally and figuratively, fell on his sword to end what had become a wretched and miserable life. If this happened today, he would have been a headliner for every news show, or even a miniseries. (If you want the whole story, see I Samuel 9–31.)

I know of no more tragic cycle of deterioration and failure than the life of Saul. It is a road map of pitfalls to avoid for anyone who wants to finish stronger than he starts. Because that's really what counts: how we finish. It doesn't matter how spectacularly we come off the starting blocks if we crash and burn before the end of the race. Our good friend Steve Farrar wrote a book a few years ago titled *Finishing Strong,* in which he uses Scripture and lively contemporary illustrations to describe what it means to build character for the long road. This topic is especially relevant for Tom and me personally. Over a decade ago, we started meeting for breakfast and dreaming of working together. We were bothered by the stories of influential people we knew who had been successful during one season of their life but fell apart in the next. So we began a partnership, not necessarily to quit our jobs and start a business enterprise—that came later. We wanted to figure out how to finish strong, to end more powerfully than we began. We didn't want to be one-season wonders.

Unfortunately, Saul's season of greatness was only momentary, and after his impressive beginning his life followed the path of a downward-spiraling staircase. He descended lower and lower, each level sending him into a phase of diminished influence until his sudden and disastrous end. We know what happened because it's documented. We know his epitaph because he spoke it himself: "Surely I have acted like a fool and have erred greatly" (I Sam 26:21b).

In medicine, influenza is an infectious disease in which a virus attacks the respiratory tract, causing a person pain, weakness, exhaustion, and general misery. It's highly contagious and can reach epidemic status quickly, resulting in widespread suffering and even death. The word *influenza* is related to the word *influence*; both terms come from the Latin verb *influere,* which means *to flow in.* We think, metaphorically speaking, influenza is an appropriate description of the process that occurs when a disorder overtakes someone's influence for good and twists it into something harmful and ugly, infecting others and leading to wide-ranging distress. Influenza is influence gone bad.

When we study the life of Saul, we can see ten clear symptoms of illness that marked his descent from influence to influenza.

UNBRIDLED SELF-INTEREST

The first attribute of a life marked by influenza is self-interest and its siblings, arrogance and uncontrolled egotism. We all have an inner self that needs to be fed if we are to maintain a healthy sense of perspective and self-respect. But we also have an ego that needs to be periodically starved to keep us from seeing ourselves as the hub around which the universe revolves. Not long after being made king, Saul started to develop a serious hub complex. Sidlow Baxter describes this stage of Saul's life well in his book *Mark These Men*: "This big-souled giant is shriveling into a shrimp. This kingly hero is becoming a toad beneath the heel of his own sadistic moods and passions. When he was little in his own eyes he was big; but the bigger he has grown in his own eyes, the less he has become."

We aren't sure exactly when and why Saul slipped off the track and began feeding his ego instead of his character. It could have been fueled by any of a number of things: insecurity, paranoia, lack of trust in God's direction. Regardless of the reason, it happened. Unbridled self-interest was Saul's first step away from positive, effective, long-term influence.

The Scriptures are full of examples of people consumed by their own self-interest. Even in the Gospels, the twelve disciples struggled with this problem while they were in their twenty-four/seven internship with Jesus. In Matthew 18 and again in Matthew 20, we read about their arguments over who was going to be the greatest in the kingdom. It was all about self-interest, and Christ had to set them straight: to be great in God's kingdom means to consider your own interests last.

Jim Collins has written two invaluable books on life and business. The first (co-authored with Jerry Porras) was titled *Built to Last* and his most recent is *Good to Great*. Both books look at successful businesses and examine the attributes that set them apart from the rest, even under unfavorable circumstances. One of those attributes is a humble leader. In *Good to Great*, Collins discusses a "Level 5 leader," a person who is an unusual mixture of humility and will, unusually modest and hesitant to talk about himself. Collins writes: "Level 5 leaders channel their ego needs away from themselves and into the larger goal of building a great company. It's not that Level 5 leaders have no ego or self interest. Indeed, they are incredibly ambitious—but their ambition is first and foremost for the institution, not themselves."

We can conclude from Collins's insights and dozens of other sources that a potent remedy for the influenza of unbridled self-interest is serving others—focusing on someone else's interests over my own. When I take my eyes off my own needs and desires and act on behalf of other people in my world, that's when my influence potential skyrockets. Of course, sometimes we delude ourselves into thinking we're being selfless when we're really just conniving and scheming for ourselves. I may tell myself I'm giving my time and energy for your good, but I really crave the praise and commendation that follows my so-called sacrifice. When our supposed generosity and servanthood are actually disguises for selfishness, our true motive inevitably escapes.

Self-interest in disguise is like a foul odor in a room that can't be masked. The other day, we discovered something in our refrigerator that was stinking up the entire kitchen, and we launched an all-out attack. We cleaned out the fridge from top to bottom, doused every kitchen surface with bleach, took the trash outside, sprayed disinfectant, and placed deodorizing agents in the room and the fridge. Even so, a whiff of the stench hung in the air for several days. In the same way, self-interest doesn't disappear without a battle—even a war. It festers, unacknowledged and hidden, until it's out of control and our appetite for attention, affirmation, and attaboys controls everything we do.

When it comes to self-interest and its effect on character and influence, perhaps the nineteenth-century minister and activist Charles Parkhurst said it best: "The man who lives by himself and for himself is likely to be corrupted by the company he keeps."

Closed-Minded Stubbornness

One of the earliest lessons we have to learn in life is to be open to other people's instruction and input. If we plant our feet and refuse to accept outside feedback, we short-circuit our influence system. Saul wrote the book on stubbornness as he began to resist input from the prophet Samuel, from other godly advisers and his family, and eventually even from God. At first he made excuses and rationalized his disobedient willfulness, but in the end his obstinacy was flagrant and at times irrationally extreme.

Whether by nature or circumstance, people who are especially susceptible to being stubborn and closed-minded tend to be founders, sole proprietors, or long-term singles. I was with a man the other day who had been very successful in starting his own company. After spending some time with him and his executive team, I began to see that no one ever disagreed with him or presented opinions contrary to his; he surrounded himself with yes men whose sole purpose was to carry out his ideas and orders. The problem with this strategy is that we all have a blind spot and bad days, which means we must have honest and forthright people who will tell us frankly when we've messed up or are about to commit a serious mistake.

Stubbornness is a subject I know very well from experience. My wife and I were married when I was twenty-nine and she was twenty-seven. In terms of habits and opinions, our union was a convergence of the Nile and the Amazon. We had each developed a way of life that suited us and had no interest in someone disrupting that lifestyle. Almost everything became grounds for an argument—do we lie in bed and flip channels for 15 minutes, read for 15 minutes, get a glass of water, and then go to sleep? Or do we do all those things in the living room, then go to bed and go to sleep right away? Do we go to the grocery store every other day, or do we carefully make a list and go once a week? Do we go to restaurants spontaneously, or do we make eating out a special occasion that we plan in advance? Eventually we realized that being stubborn only led to frustration—and we influenced each other very little when we dug our heels in.

Being stubborn also prevents us from being teachable, and when we lose the ability to learn, we stop influencing for good. Cultivating a teachable spirit should start early in life, which is why the book of Proverbs tells fathers to teach their children the art of receiving instruction: "Listen, my sons, to a father's instruction; pay attention and gain understanding" (Proverbs 4:1). "Stop listening to instruction, my son, and you will stray from the words of knowledge" (Proverbs 19:27).

Though my wife and I have learned (and are still learning) to be flexible and open to each other's input, the roots of obstinate independence run deep and strong in our soil—and the apples have not fallen far from the tree. We have had to target stubbornness as a primary focus in our kids so that they can grow up to be healthy influencers themselves and not be cut down by the kind of blind inflexibility that crippled Saul.

RASH IMPULSIVENESS

People who act rashly develop a reputation for not thinking matters through and for changing their mind quickly. This lack of consistency makes it difficult for others to place trust and confidence in them, which hurts their position of influence. The other extreme is someone who can't engage, who thinks and thinks but never acts—the Hamlet syndrome. That behavior certainly has its disadvantages where influence is concerned. But Saul had the opposite problem: rash impulsiveness.

Saul acted hastily and recklessly on a number of occasions, overruling God's timing and authority. Samuel told him to wait to offer a sacrifice after defeating the Ammonites, but he became impatient and took the task into his own hands. In a later incident, Saul rashly imposed a death penalty on any man who ate before Saul avenged himself on his enemies (I Sam 14:18–27). That hasty edict weakened his army and would have sentenced his own son to death if the people had not stepped in on Jonathan's behalf.

An impulsive and reckless nature usually leads to lots of regret, second-guessing, and involvement in matters that look good at first but eventually tarnish. Saul's impulsive and erratic behavior ended up costing him and his heirs the kingdom; that's quite a loss of influence.

ISOLATION *and* SECRECY

Another symptom of Saul's influenza was his refusal to take advantage of the sound, healthy friends and counselors with whom he was surrounded. God assigned Samuel to come alongside Saul for accountability and encouragement. But Saul became too busy, too important, too self-oriented, too distant, too dishonest, and too insensitive to benefit from Samuel's friendship, and eventually the relationship was broken. Later in life, David's music and company soothed Saul's troubled spirit, but murderous suspicion and fear drove that companionship away as well.

Men and women in a leadership position often believe that no one understands the issues and challenges they face; they can be particularly prone to the perils of isolation. One of my friends is dealing with the consequences of a devastating phase of life in which he had an extramarital affair that ended his marriage. By his own account, the single factor that most contributed to his moral failure was that he began to withdraw from accountability relationships and become secretive. He didn't return calls, didn't answer messages. He cut off the people who would ask the hard questions and help him tackle the difficult issues. In that vacuum, danger was unavoidable.

We all need a handful of confidants with whom we can process life. We were never intended to live as the lone ranger. We need community, no matter what it looks like. Without it, no one influences us for the better and we have no one to influence.

USING PEOPLE *for* PERSONAL GAIN

Another manifestation of influenza is actually an outgrowth of self-interest, but it deserves a category all its own because of its devastating impact on personal influence. I know I have been guilty of manipulating people for my own benefit, and I think most of us would admit to having done it at one time or another. Saul elevated this process to an art form, until few relationships were untainted by his selfish motivation. Not even his own family was spared. Driven by hatred and fear of David, Saul used both his son Jonathan and his daughter Michal to try to end David's life and eliminate the perceived threat to his throne.

During the five years we were the stewards of Life@Work (our company, dedicated to helping people integrate their faith and their professional lives), we were privileged to work with an incredible number of men and women of faith across the country. But we made an observation and learned a lesson early. From the outset, we had people of amazing influence put their clout to work on behalf of our undertaking, with no expectation of anything in return. One such person was Bob Briner, a tremendous spokesman for the faith-work movement and the author of *Roaring Lambs*, a catalyst in generating conversation about the subject for the last ten years. Bob has had an incredible influence on a number of men and women, and at the outset of Life@Work we called him out of the clear blue to ask for his input in our enterprise. To our joy, he responded with grace and open arms. We made a pilgrimage to Greenville, Illinois, where Bob was a college professor. He spent several days with us then and numerous hours on the phone with us afterward, helping us shape and understand the world of faith and work without a shred of expectation of personal gain. Bob has since passed away, but the selfless generosity of his life continues to be part of his ongoing legacy to us and countless others.

Another individual who leaned into the Life@Work effort was Bob Buford, author of the book *Halftime* and (like Bob Briner) a pioneer of the faith-work movement. Bob had developed key relationships in this area all over the country, and he let us use his list of contacts to spread awareness of Life@Work. He'd never done this before, and it made a huge difference in our getting the word out. Both these men, and many other individuals, shamelessly got behind our wagon and helped us pushed Life@Work without wanting anything in return.

But as we got off the ground, an interesting thing happened. Our phone began ringing off the wall with people interested in working with us or associating with us. Without fail, they fell into two categories: those who expected to benefit personally, and those who didn't. We developed a sixth sense that allowed us to spot someone with selfish motivation in fifteen seconds. In their attitude, their language, and their questions, they seemed to be saying, "If I attach myself to this endeavor, it will be good for me." We tried to avoid working with these people, and this is often the result of using people as a tool for self-advancement. We may think we can use people to expand our influence, but in the end this kind of behavior only diminishes our clout.

KNOWINGLY DOING WRONG

Shortly into his reign, Saul began to become deceitful and disobedient to God. It began with isolated incidents, but soon outright rebellion was his habit and lifestyle. We can see the beginning of this cycle in I Samuel 15, when God, through the prophet Samuel, tells Saul to completely destroy the Amalekites. Saul instead spares the Amalekite king and the best livestock. When Samuel challenges Saul, he argues, rationalizes his behavior, shifts the blame to his soldiers, and then tries to twist the entire episode into a sacrifice and worship experience. It doesn't work, and God takes the kingdom away from Saul.

Knowingly doing wrong is evidence of a steady downward regression toward influenza. It begins with small things and progresses until eventually we have a hard time telling right from wrong; the line becomes blurred. It's not really blurred, but we can't see it clearly anymore. This process chips away at our ethos—our believability—in large part because it erodes our self-respect. There's something refueling to the spirit about a moral victory. Doing the right thing creates an aroma of attractiveness to others and establishes the moral foundation for our ability to influence.

FAILURE *to* DEAL *with* UNRESOLVED CONFLICT

Saul turned into a self-destructive wrecking crew by sabotaging his personal relationships and avoiding resolution of conflict, which was devastating for his personal influence. He developed a petty jealousy of young David, which turned into a full-blown hurricane of malice and revenge once David's popularity overshadowed that of Saul. When they returned from battle, the people sang in the streets, "Saul has slain his thousands and David his tens of thousands" (I Samuel 18:7). Saul's jealousy became so extreme that he tried to kill David three times.

In the New Testament, Jesus addresses interpersonal conflict and how it should be handled:

Therefore, if you are offering your gift at the altar and there remember that your brother has something against you, leave your gift there in front of the altar. First go and be reconciled to your brother; then come and offer your gift. Settle matters quickly with your adversary who is taking you to court. Do it while you are still with him on the way, or he may hand you over to the judge, and the judge may hand you over to the officer, and you may be thrown into prison. I tell you the truth, you will not get out until you have paid the last penny.

You have heard that it was said, "Eye for eye, and tooth for tooth." But I tell you, Do not resist an evil person. If someone strikes you on the right cheek, turn to him the other also. And if someone wants to sue you and take your tunic, let him have your cloak as well. If someone forces you to go one mile, go with him two miles. Give to the one who asks you, and do not turn away from the one who wants to borrow from you [Matthew 5:23–26, 38–42].

From these verses we can draw several principles of relational restoration:

• *Make relational harmony a high priority.* This means addressing conflict quickly and not allowing discord to gain a foothold. Ephesians 4:26 says, "Do not let the sun go down while you are still angry."
• *Take the initiative in reconciliation.* It doesn't matter whether you did the harming or were harmed. We can't make conflict go away by ignoring it.
• *Avoid revenge at all cost.* Charles Swindoll, in his book *Joseph: From Pit to Pinnacle*, gives us from the life of Joseph a glimpse of how we should handle people who harm us:

No one who does a serious study of Joseph's life would deny that he was a great man. And yet he never accomplished any of the things we normally associate with biblical greatness. He never slew a giant. He never wrote a line of Scripture or made any vast prophetic predictions like Daniel. Come to think of it, Joseph never even performed a single miracle. He was just your typical boy next door who grew up in a very troubled family.

So what made Joseph great? Why does God devote more space in Genesis to his story than to any other patriarch? Because of Joseph's attitude, how he responded to difficult circumstances. That was the most remarkable thing about him.

American author Elbert Hubbard once wrote, "The final proof of greatness lies in being able to endure contemptuous treatment without resentment." Joseph spent a good deal of his life enduring hardship, hateful treatment, and his attitude during those years offers indisputable proof of his greatness.

If anyone had justification for revenge, it was Joseph. But he didn't seek it, and God honored him for it. An attitude of vengefulness consumes our energy and drains our relationships. It cuts our influence platform out from under us and leaves us with nothing but solitude and empty bitterness.

• *Go the second mile in forgiveness and kindness.* Addressing conflict gives us the opportunity not only to mend the damage but to make the relationship even stronger.

PARALYSIS *with* PAST FAILURE

As we discussed in Chapter Six, we all experience failure; it's unavoidable. But how we handle that failure determines whether our influence suffers or grows as a result of it. A serious hindrance to our clout is inability to move on. We become fixated on the failure instead of accepting God's ready forgiveness and mercy. Saul experienced failure but couldn't shake it.

We all fail, but we don't have to be paralyzed by it. We have to deal with it and move on, as Paul says, "forgetting what is behind you and straining toward what is ahead" (Philippians 3:13). Forgetting doesn't mean denying wrongdoing and failure. But after we accept it and deal with it, we move on down the road with renewed purpose and conviction. Steve Farrar, in *Finishing Strong,* quotes the famous abolitionist and minister Henry Ward Beecher: "It is defeat that turns bone to flint, and gristle to muscle, and makes people invincible, and forms those heroic natures that are now in ascendancy in the world. Do not, then, be afraid of defeat. You are never so near to victory as when defeated in a good cause."

INABILITY *to* EFFECT TRANSITION LEADERSHIP

One thing that put Saul on the fast track downward was his refusal to accept that someone else would be the next king of Israel. It literally drove him crazy, until he was hurling spears at shadows in corners. Although Saul took this lack of transitional ability to an extreme, it has plagued many a leader's influence. Founders especially seem to have trouble with transition.

I know of a founder of a national ministry (not a household name) who outlived his effectiveness and would not pass the baton at the appointed time. It was obvious to everyone but him that it needed to happen, but the people who brought this up to him eventually found themselves cut off. The entrenched leader brought in new faces who would tell him that he still "had it." This leader ended up destroying much of what he had built in his years of peak influence.

A leader's refusal to let someone else take the reins is common, but it happens regularly in churches, nonprofit organizations, universities, and first-generation companies. This type of organization is often centered on someone who has enough wealth or vision to build a self-generating organization; that position can be especially difficult to transition out of.

RELIANCE *on* DEATH *to* RESOLVE LIFE'S MISTAKES

Though he battled them all his life, the Philistines were not Saul's worst enemy. Saul himself was his own worst enemy. When he came up against the wall at the end of his life and saw no hope, no chance to undo the wrong he had done and caused, the downward spiral of his life that led to the death of his own sons, he took the only option he could think of: he fell on his sword to end his life.

Using death as a last-ditch effort is not always as dramatic as Saul's action, but it is still quite common. Many people hope that on their dying day they can spread money around to cover their wrongs and reverse the direction their influence took during life. Many people write a letter on their deathbed hoping it will act as a magic bullet to put everything right. It rarely works. The time to have influence is during life.

MODERN-DAY SAULS

The story of Saul's downfall was quite visible and has been recorded as a warning for all students of the Bible. Not all of us show our symptoms so clearly, but they are there nonetheless. Some of the worst cases of influenza are found in the same place as the best examples of influence: the church, the family, sports, the classroom. For many people, these areas of life are an anchor for positive, healthy influence. Many who are asked to identify the top influencers in their life would name a minister, a parent, a coach, or a teacher. However, for others, these are the very sources from which influenza is contracted.

Recent disclosures of sexual abuse in the Catholic church and the repressive legalism of some fundamentalist churches are evidence of the diseased people within. The same goes for the family, when a parent, a sibling, or another relative abuses trust and does and says horrible things to another member. Some coaches have been known to verbally or physically abuse their players or resort to other damaging methods in an attempt to win at all costs. When a teacher violates the trust and integrity of a teacher-student relationship or fails to tap into a student's motivation, positive influence unravels.

The pages of modern history tell of one of the most chilling cases of influenza ever, in which unchecked evil introduced itself in human form and overshadowed the lives of Russia's Czar Nicholas II and his wife, Alexandra, and eventually the whole empire.

Nicholas II and Alexandra desperately wanted a son and an heir, but not long after their boy was born, they learned that he had hemophilia, a deadly blood disease that could snatch his life away at any time. Doctors could do little for the boy, and the czar and his wife lived in constant fear of their son's death. Into this sorrowful situation stepped Grigori Rasputin, an uneducated peasant who dabbled in mysticism and shady religious practices that combined spiritual fervor with sexual indulgence. He prayed for the boy, and to everyone's surprise the boy improved dramatically, though temporarily. Again Rasputin prayed, and again the child rallied. Even today the nature of these healings is not understood, but they are documented by multiple historical sources. They solidly locked in Rasputin's clout with the royal family, especially with Alexandra.

Rasputin claimed that the heir to the throne would live only so long as Alexandra complied with his orders. His influence became so strong that he could bring about approval or dismissal of any individual in the government. If someone expressed suspicion about Rasputin's role, he was tossed out of court and replaced with an appointee whose unscrupulousness and greed matched Rasputin's own. As a result, the entire political system lurched under the influence of this unwise and evil man, who came to be known as the Mad Monk of Russia. Eventually the empire fell into chaos, setting the stage for a bloody revolution that resulted in the murder of the royal family and ultimately the establishment of the communist coup. Some have speculated that if Rasputin's corrupt influence had not entered the picture, Lenin could not have come to power.

We hope there aren't many Rasputins-in-the-making out there, but this story is a disquieting reminder of the dangers in allowing influenza to go unchecked and untreated. Chaos and destruction, whether of the spirit or an entire empire, are often the result.

• • •

Key Points

- We metaphorically use the word *influenza*, which is related to *influence* (remember that the Latin *influere* means to flow in) to describe influence gone bad. With good influence, the positive traits of one person flow into another individual. With bad influence, the negative traits of one person flow into another, just as an infectious influenza virus attacks the respiratory system.

- Influenza is characterized by one or more of these traits:

    Unbridled self-interest. Arrogance and uncontrolled egotism are incredibly unattractive to people around us; both personal experience and research prove those traits to be anathema to the good-influence process.

Closed-minded stubbornness. If we plant our feet and refuse to accept outside feedback, we short-circuit the influence system.

Rash impulsiveness. People have trouble trusting or placing their confidence in someone who has a reputation for not thinking matters through or changing mind and direction quickly.

Isolation and secrecy. We need other people around us to do life well, in terms of accountability and encouragement. Men and women who pull back and withdraw from this kind of positive relationship compromise their ability to be a positive influence.

Using people for personal gain. Manipulating people for inappropriate personal benefit and gain is devastating to the perpetrator and the target.

Knowingly doing wrong. Deceit and willful disobedience often begins with small things and over time progresses into a full downward spiral. It is not good to be around people evidencing this pattern of behavior; the process consistently erodes their ethos and ability to influence positively.

Failure to deal with unresolved conflict. Avoiding resolution of conflict sabotages personal relationships and makes positive influence difficult. Scripture recommends (1) making relational harmony a high priority, (2) taking the initiative in reconciliation, (3) avoiding revenge, and (4) going the extra mile in forgiveness and kindness.

Paralysis with past failure. Failure is unavoidable, but how we deal with it makes all the difference in whether, and how, our influence grows.

Inability to effect transition in leadership. A leader's refusal to let someone else take the reins—or admit that sooner or later he or she will no longer be in the leadership position— is a common malady that dials the influence meter down.

Reliance on death to resolve life's mistakes. If we believe that money to be distributed or the plans to be executed on our death will solve what we are unable to confront while living, we are kidding ourselves about the extent of our positive influence.

Class-Seven Influence

10,585 Days and Counting

Life must be understood backwards. But . . . it must be lived forwards.

—Søren Kierkegaard

A FEW NIGHTS AGO, I SAT AT OUR KITCHEN table and turned my family into a five-person focus group. We were all home, everyone was in a good mood, and there were no commitments that night to turn dinner into a fast-food-at-home experience. (You know what that is: an evening where everyone races to choke down their food, and then the group scatters like a covey of quail with a burst of sound and activity.) It was the end of the summer, and all eyes were starting to look ahead to the school year. The impending transition prompted some talk of the summer gone by and the year ahead. It was a perfect context for me to casually ask my family, "Who is it that's had the greatest influence on you in the last twelve months?"

One by one, we all answered the question. There were one or two surprises, but nothing shocking. Everyone seemed to have a little energy and interest left, so I followed up with, "What have they done that makes you say that?" That's when it got interesting—to have these influence customers pull the curtain back for the rest of us to see how the process worked.

Back in 1997, in late summer, two world-renowned women passed from this life to the next within eight days of each other. Princess Diana of Wales was tall, slender, and striking; she carried a royal glow about her. Mother Teresa of Calcutta was short, aged, and frail; she seemed to be illuminated from within by a divine radiance. Every newspaper, magazine, television, and radio station in the world carried the stories of their deaths, and many followed up in the ensuing months with analysis and deliberation about the meaning and impact of their lives. Some drew comparisons between the two.

One commentator said Princess Di and Mother Teresa were two of the top ten female world-changers in the last two hundred years. That's a pretty lofty statement; it made me wonder who compiled that list and who else was on it. But then I thought a little deeper, and I asked a more important question: What does someone *do*—what are the activities and habits—that land a person on a list of world-class influencers?

World-class is a high-water mark for any endeavor. Have you ever taken a canoe, kayak, or raft over a set of class-four rapids? These are long stretches of fast-moving water requiring powerful and precise maneuvering. If you've been in the hands of an expert guide through waters like this, or if you're skilled enough to navigate them yourself, you know that it's a rush of excitement and a thrill. A world-class influencer is about that rare and that exciting. Let's call such a person a class-seven influencer. Here's why I suggest that.

First, seven has been referred to as the perfect number. Now, I'm not into excessive numerology; I don't even know much about it. But I do know that numerology attaches special significance to certain numbers and patterns. According to those who study numbers in a mystical way, seven is special because it contains all the things of heaven (symbolized by the number three) and all the things of earth (symbolized by the number four) in perfect convergence. This reminds me of the movie *The Perfect Storm*, which came out on the big screen in 2000 and was based on the book by Sebastian Junger. The movie and book tell the true story of a fishing boat that had the misfortune to be hit by three storms that combined into one: an Atlantic Nor'easter, a subtropical low-pressure system, and the remnants of

Hurricane Grace. There was no meteorological category for this unprecedented convergence of weather systems, so it simply became known as "the perfect storm." At its nightmarish center, it generated waves up to one hundred feet high—as tall as a ten-story building.

As with a perfect storm, has there ever been a perfect model of influence, someone in whom all the elements converged for results that shattered history? The best example I can think of is Jesus. He topped Aristotle's Triangle; He had a message that was meaningful, a life that was believable, and an audience that (if not always receptive) certainly couldn't ignore Him.

We've devoted a chapter to Jesus already. But that was a conceptual, theoretical approach. That was our asking Jesus the question, "What do you *think* about influence?" Here we're looking at something different. We're asking Jesus, "How did you *do* influence?" We are asking the same question I did of my kids and the same deeper question that we asked about Mother Teresa and Princess Di. What did the influencers *do* that resulted in such extraordinary outcomes?

Jesus tops the list of the most influential figures to walk the earth and has held that rank for twenty centuries running. He did it in large part through training twelve unlikely candidates to be world-class influencers themselves—and He was with them for only three years. The results of their three-year apprenticeship with Jesus are staggering. We want to look at what He did that we can imitate and apply to our own world of influence.

We've talked about a lot in this book. Let's bring it down to the essentials and identify seven elements from the life of Jesus that, when combined, create a once-in-a-lifetime, world-class influence experience.

INFLUENCE *from the* BASE *of* GENUINE FRIENDSHIP

We've already learned that each of us has an oikos, or multiple spheres of influence that are a ready-made arena for us to make an impact. These are the natural highways of our lives; there's no need to go off-roading for influence opportunities. Genuine friendship is one of the most natural avenues for us to make a difference.

We're not suggesting that everyone you know become an intimate best friend. According to Jerry and Mary White, authors of *Friends and Friendship*, our relationships fall into the categories of acquaintance, casual friend, close friend, and intimate best friend. There's no way everyone in our sphere can be classified as close and intimate. Common sense and experience say that the higher we go in the friendship pyramid, the fewer the people at each level. The Whites make the case that if we can establish three to five deep and intimate friendships, we've achieved something significant.

I've said it before: I'm convinced that Jesus really liked the twelve disciples. His time with them wasn't just a job that forced Him to put up with people who got on His nerves. I am further convinced that Jesus practiced all the relational dynamics we talk about in today's high-RQ (relational quotient) culture. He and the disciples had fun together; they shared interests, mutual trust, and natural chemistry. We know Jesus valued the concept of friendship because of what He says in the book of John: "My command is this: Love each other as I have loved you. Greater love has no one than this, that he lay down his life for his friends. You are my friends if you do what I command. I no longer call you servants, because a servant does not know his master's business. Instead, I have called you friends, for everything that I learned from my Father I have made known to you" (John 15:12–15).

Jesus called the disciples (and other New Testament characters) His friends. As a matter of fact, people often said of Him, "Here is . . . a friend of tax collectors and sinners" (Matt. 11:19). Jesus was a miracle worker, an amazing teacher of truth, and a compelling story-teller—but He was also a friend. It was from this platform that Jesus worked His greatest influence.

One of the best places to build a friendship is at work. Some say this is a no-no, but I don't agree. The workplace is a place of shared interests, passions, and goals; the base for friendship is often already there—we just have to build on it. How do we do it? By doing what Jesus did. He approached people, asked questions, and showed interest. An easy place to start is with a smile. I wish smiles were more contagious in our society. When we go to a meeting, approach a ticket counter, walk into a restaurant, or show up at church, doesn't receiving a genuine, warm smile change our entire mood? We can do that for someone else just by exercising a few facial muscles. To put it in Aristotelian terms, a smile transforms pathos. To put it in biblical terms, "A cheerful look brings joy to the heart" (Proverbs 15:30).

A few years ago, my wife and I went to an out-of-town basketball game. We happened to be part of a caravan that stopped after the game at a run-down local hamburger joint, where the food quality pretty much matched the decor. We ended up clustering tables together. Sitting at our table was a group of people who went to the same church and seemed to be good friends with each other. Because we were a large group, it took the waitperson more than two hours to serve us. But for my wife and me, it seemed even longer. Not one person asked us a question as we sat nose to nose for two hours. No one even acknowledged that we were there. On the way home, I told my wife that I hoped I never made anyone feel like an outsider the way that group made me feel that night. Asking someone about themselves is about as basic as it gets. It's Being Friendly Baby Steps 101. My kids know it. Even my chocolate lab Duke knows it.

A friendly smile and a friendly attitude are basic building blocks in the influence process. They lead to significant, even intimate friendships that can transform lives for the better.

This is the power of a friendly smile in the influence process.

EXPAND *the* PERSONAL VISION *of* THOSE AROUND YOU

When Jesus looked at Peter and Andrew, He saw more than fishermen. He knew they had the skills necessary to sail the wind-blown, storm-battered lakes of Galilee and bring back fish, but He also knew they would go out in the world and make disciples. So He challenged them with a life-altering vision. He said, "Peter, I think you could be a fisher of men. Andrew, I think you can reharness your skills for the kingdom." Jesus invented the value-added concept; He added the eternal to their daily. That's vision, and we can do the same thing for people in our lives. Here are some transferable principles Jesus offers us on vision.

Vision Must Be Inspiring

I am asked all the time what it takes for people to change in today's culture. The answer is threefold: they need information, inspiration, and affiliation. Many people stop at information. That's important; a meaningful message is essential. But people need more than that. The best influencers bring inspiration to work with them—not in their briefcase, but in their skin. They are inspiration incarnate.

Vision Must Be Believable

I have often wondered if Jesus looked at Peter through all of his short-comings and fumbles and saw the book of Acts—the miracles, sermons, and ground-breaking church leadership. When Jesus told Peter he would become the foundation of the church, He wasn't just pumping him up with empty talk. He knew what the Spirit would enable him to do, and He wanted Peter to believe that vision too. Some time back, I found myself sitting across from an adrenaline-charged, fast-talking, superlative-slinging salesman. My business partner and I met with this tornado of a human being in a coffee shop in Los Angeles for an hour. At the end of his talk, I felt worn out by a whole lot of nothing. This man was all storefront. We looked through the door and saw nothing behind it. When we believe in people, we can't just inflate them with empty enthusiasm. If their reality doesn't match our glorious gusto, they come crashing down, worse off than before.

Vision Must Be Personal

If we want to really make a difference in people's lives, we have to be observant and help them see beyond themselves. I'm often surprised by the effect we can have just by noticing and commenting on a unique talent or character trait. At one point a while back, a friend jotted me a thank-you note. It was one of the best notes I've ever received. I read it out loud to my wife and said, "This guy has an incredible way with words." The next time I saw my friend, I told him what I thought. It wasn't hot air; it was believable. It was personal. I asked him if he'd ever thought about writing, and he has since been writing poems and short stories. Tom Clancy, look out!

Many people think vision is mystical and cosmic, that it descends on you from out of nowhere in a flash of illumination. Sometimes vision happens this way, but it's rare. Expanding someone's vision is as simple as getting our eyes off ourselves and paying attention to a person long enough to see something great, and then help them make that greatness a reality.

This is the power of visioning in the influence process.

STAY ANCHORED *to* YOUR OWN MISSION *and* CALLING

Jesus never lost His compass, but it's amazing how easy it is for us to lose our sense of direction. In the effort to influence others, or even just traveling through life, we may lose our anchor. If we become wobbly in our own sense of calling, it's difficult to help other people with theirs.

Naturally, staying anchored to a mission means knowing what the mission is. In the strategic life coaching part of our consulting practice, we love to help people discover and articulate their calling. We define calling as God's personal invitation for us to work on His agenda, using the talents we've been given in a way that is eternally significant. Calling involves asking and answering four questions, some of the greatest questions in life:

1. Origin: Where did I come from?
2. Purpose: Why am I here?
3. Identity: Who am I?
4. Eternity: Where am I going?

If we can work through those questions by writing down our thoughts, making a list, talking with folks who will be honest with us, seeking insight from a trusted counselor with greater maturity and experience, and then refining and reshaping our answers, a picture of who we truly are begins to emerge, and from this picture we begin to see our calling. Crafting a personal statement of calling and mission helps us see what we were created to do and where our potential for greatness lies. Someone who has nailed down her personal calling sees more clearly to influence others than someone who is flailing about, directionless in his life. (For more help on this subject, see our book *A Case for Calling*.)

When Jesus was astonishing the teachers of the law in the temple at age twelve (Luke 2:46), receiving the blessing of God the Father at His baptism (Matthew 3:17), or turning His face toward Jerusalem

(Luke 9:51), He was staying true and centered in His own mission and calling. Even as He was pouring His life into other people, He was clear and focused on His own purpose and assignment.

Like Jesus, when we are secure in our personal mission and calling, our ethos—the believability of our life—is a beacon. We are like a lighthouse on the coast that guides weary, lost travelers. Our simple presence has tremendous influence for people within its scope because of the light of confidence, peace, and clarity that shines forth.

This is the power of calling in the influence process.

MODEL PERSONAL SPIRITUAL VITALITY

When looking at the life of Jesus, we find a question: How did Jesus keep personal vitality in His faith and relationships? How was He not stretched into nothing and pulled to pieces by all those who were making demands on Him: the crowds, the disciples, the sick and dying, the religious leaders? The answer is that He took care of the depth and let God take care of the breadth. We can do the same. That means we concentrate on the message that's meaningful and the life that's believable, and let God figure out how wide and far the ripples of our influence extend.

Remember the scene of Mary and Martha? Martha was busy in the kitchen while Mary sat at the feet of Jesus, soaking up His presence. Martha was worn out by her duties and became resentful, and Jesus had to gently remind her that she was ignoring the source of spiritual vitality—Him—as she poured her energy into inconsequential tasks. How many times do we pour out our strength on things that don't matter instead of receiving it from God? We can receive and spend our spiritual vitality foolishly or wisely.

There is a hierarchy in a well-ordered life. The vertical relationship, our connection with God, should be first, and the horizontal, that with other people, should be second. If they get out of order, problems follow. I learned early in my theology studies that many religious systems are built around a horizontal model; they emphasize doing over being and are directed first to people and then to God. Jesus said the teachings of Scripture can all be rolled into one sentence: "Love the Lord your God with all your heart and with all your soul and with all your strength and with all your mind, and love your neighbor as yourself"

(Luke 10:27). Maintaining our spiritual vitality, and showcasing that vertical relationship, should be a cornerstone for us.

This is the power of modeling in the process of influence.

GIVE PEOPLE ROOM *to* GROW

After Jesus enlisted the twelve, they failed many times and in many ways. He asked them to be servants, and they argued about which one would be the greatest. He asked them to pray during a painful time, and they fell asleep. He asked them to be peaceful, and one of them hacked off a soldier's ear. He asked them to stand up with Him, and they slithered into anonymity, even denying any connection. These weren't freshman mistakes in the disciples' first year of internship. They were heading toward graduation. We don't know if Jesus ever experienced a moment of frustration. I know I would have.

But Jesus didn't tell the disciples they were terrible, fire them from the discipleship club, recruit another twelve, and let everyone know how easily they could be replaced. Jesus patiently let them grow and gave them some slack—especially Peter, who may have disappointed Jesus the most. When we read the gospels, we see Jesus giving the disciples rope, then evaluation, then more rope, then more evaluation, then more rope.

My wife is better at this than I am. She has taught me a great deal about letting people grow. She is a master in the kitchen cooking with our kids. They try and they fail, but they can't wait to get back into the game after her patient encouragement.

In the game of influence, we must let people grow and develop. We can't expect overnight results. Like a river carving out a new path in the landscape, we have to let water and time do their job in the influence process.

This is the power of grace in the influence process.

INJECT INTENTIONALITY WHEN APPROPRIATE

You bet I'm saying we should have an agenda in our influence! The people who have influenced me the most in my life all made a very clear point of it, and we should make a point of it in the people we seek to influence. We should see the opportunity, make a plan, and follow through on it. Of course, not every situation calls for deployment of the whole armed services. Sometimes we just need to patiently keep lighting and salting, doing the right thing, and wait.

But sometimes there's a chance to be much more direct—to be a mentor. Raising morally responsible and biblically responsive children takes the help of all those who will join the construction team. No parent I know of would reject help from someone genuinely interested in seeing their child grow. Families need all the help they can get. In keeping ourselves on the straight and narrow, we need all the help we can get. In holding a company to high standards of ethics and excellence, a boss needs all the help he or she can get. In helping students learn to use their minds and develop discipline, a teacher needs all the help she or he can get. There is no shortage of opportunities to influence if we just have the eyes to intentionally see them.

This is the power of intentionality in the influence process.

Don't Overcontrol Outcomes

Our definition of influence is shaping people and outcomes. But we must be careful to take a long-term approach to the results and let God and timing do their work. We must also account for the mystery that sometimes takes the results out of our hands. Being a significant influence in the world means having an attitude of patience and acceptance, not power and control.

This principle doesn't affect us until we are truly engaged in the influence agenda. It is after a parent decides to really deposit meaningful life-skills and lessons into a child that expectations rise. It is after two people have agreed to a coaching/mentoring relationship that expectations rise. It is after a boss determines to groom a certain employee for a promotion that expectations begin to mount. We must ride straddled between "no expectations, no disappointments" and "expect the best, get the best." The ride is often an uneasy one, for even the most seasoned influence cowboy.

This is the power of patience in the influence process.

Be *an* Influence Bigfoot

We all have a significant chance to plant a footprint of influence in the sand. At a board meeting I attended several years ago, the chairperson opened with a devotional, and the verse chosen was Psalm

90:12: "Teach us to number our days aright, that we may gain a heart of wisdom." That verse triggered this man's thinking. He used the average life span of an American male—78.6 years—to calculate the number of days he had left in life. I have done the same calculation, and I have 10,585 days left in life as of this writing. I have an opportunity to bring a positive, effective, appropriate influence to bear in every sphere I walk. Margaret Lee Runbeck comments on this (in *Draper's Book of Quotations*): "A man leaves all kinds of footprints when he walks through life. Some you can see, like his children and his house. Others are invisible, like the print he leaves across other people's lives—the help he gives them and what he has said, his jokes, gossip that has hurt others, encouragement. We don't think about it, but everywhere we pass, we leave some kind of mark."

I want to make a giant step in the sand with my influence; I want to be an influence bigfoot. We all have seven days a week and twelve months a year to influence other people. James gives us a sobering reminder of how brief our time is: "Now listen, you who say, 'Today or tomorrow we will go to this or that city, spend a year there, carry on business and make money.' Why, you do not even know what will happen tomorrow. What is your life? You are a mist that appears for a little while and then vanishes. Instead, you ought to say, 'If it is the Lord's will, we will live and do this or that'" (James 4:13–15).

What does James mean, "this or that"? We submit that it could be influence; if it is the Lord's will, we will influence others. This and that is the bare minimum of what we do. Whatever else qualifies, at the least we should be influencing other people.

Dave Roper, in his book *Seeing Through*, helps us get a handle on the finish line:

So you're not a major player. So you have no political clout or power base. So you're not a Christian quarterback, a converted rock star, a multi-media personality, or a multi-millionaire.

You can be a catalyst for change.

You can be used to arrest the spread of corruption in your community.

You can be a source of light in your dark corner of society.

You can be the means by which some part of our crazy world is brought into sync.

We are all designed to be of incalculable use to God. He planned our usefulness before time began. "We are God's workmanship," Paul insists, "created in Christ Jesus to do good works, which God prepared in advance for us to do." (Ephesians 2:10)

Perhaps it will be a visible role; more likely it's concealed and hidden. It could be that your entire light will find its meaning in one person whom God wants you to touch in some significant way—in one event in which he yearns to make himself known.

Planting *for* Eternity

The year was 1986; the place was Montana. Specifically, it was the breathtaking Elk Canyon Ranch Lodge, three hours from Bozeman. Four men, businesspeople and best friends from Dallas, were spending a few quick days with three dozen other men and James Dobson for a spiritual retreat. Hugo Schoellkopf III was a successful businessman in Dallas and owner of the Montana ranch. George Clark was chairman and CEO of M Bank and one of Dallas's most prominent civic boosters. Trevor Mayberry was an ENT surgeon and on the staff of Humana Hospital in Dallas. Creath Davis was a minister who spent his time discipling businessmen in Dallas.

On Sunday morning, Hugo and his friends climbed into his six-seat twin-engine plane for the six-hour flight back to Dallas. It should have been a routine 1,250-mile flight from White Sulfur Springs to Addison, a trip Hugo had made dozens and dozens of times. When the plane failed to arrive Sunday afternoon, an aggressive air search began. It lasted until Wednesday, when a civil air patrol pilot spotted a glacier that didn't look right. The Cessna had crashed into its slope; the men were killed instantly.

The tragedy shook Dallas and beyond. The funeral services were held at Park City Baptist Church, where Howard Hendricks, Clayton Bell, and James Dobson presided. President Ronald Reagan sent a long telegram, and the place was packed. The seats were jammed with men and women whom these four men had influenced and touched. They had wielded the right kind of clout, which yielded the right kind of harvest. They had lived a class-seven life of influence. Looking at the front row at the very end of the service, Jim Dobson delivered a final message to the children of the men.

With a breaking voice, he said, "You kids had great men for fathers. They were great not because of what they accomplished or achieved or accumulated. They were great because of the way they lived their lives and influenced others. Great because of the way they loved, great because of the way they gave, and great because of the way they served."

Greatness and influence are inherently linked. But, as these men demonstrated and Dobson pointed out, true greatness, and true influence, are found in making others great. This is when class-seven influence is in full force: when one lone person determines to be salt and light and leave the results to God. When a lone person determines that a significant part of his or her calling in this life is to influence correctly. Then the class-seven thrill ride begins. We are not planting seeds that shoot up overnight and then shrivel away. We are planting seeds for cross-generational harvesting. Grab a pair of overalls, a few tools, and meet us out in the field.

● ● ●

Key Points

- A class-seven influencer influences from a base of genuine friendship. Genuine friendship is one of the most natural avenues for us to make a difference.

- A class-seven influencer expands the personal vision of those around us. Helping others better understand how they can make a magnified difference allows influence to leverage good in the life of another. The vision must be inspiring, believable, and personal.

- A class-seven influencer remains anchored to his or her own mission and calling. People who influence others do so only if they keep their own bearing.

- A class-seven influencer models personal spiritual vitality. Jesus kept spiritual vitality by continuing to cultivate a deep relationship with God the Father, and letting God take care of the breadth of Christ's influence. We concentrate on a message that is believable and a life that is meaningful, and we allow God to determine how far and wide the ripples of our influence extend.

- A class-seven influencer gives people room to grow. Jesus gave His disciples rope, then evaluation, then rope, then evaluation. Being influential means allowing people to grow and develop over time.

- A class-seven influencer injects intentionality. People who influence greatly have an intentional agenda for their work with others.

- A class-seven influencer avoids overcontrolling outcomes. Being a significant influence means having an attitude of patience and acceptance, not power and control.

- We have the opportunity to be an influence bigfoot, the kind of person who leaves prints in the sand for others to step in as they make their way through life.

References

Baxter, Sidlow. *Mark These Men: Practical Studies in Striking Aspects of Certain Bible Characters.* Grand Rapids, Mich.: Zondervan, 1960.

Briner, Bob. *Roaring Lambs: A Gentle Plan to Radically Change Our World.* Grand Rapids, Mich.: Zondervan, 1993.

Buford, Bob. *Halftime: Changing Your Game Plan from Success to Significance.* Grand Rapids, Mich.: Zondervan, 1994.

Coleman, Robert. *The Master Plan of Evangelism.* Westwood, N.J.: F. H. Revell, 1964.

Collins, Eliza, and Patricia Scott. "Everyone Who Makes It Has a Mentor." *Harvard Business Review,* vol. 56, pp. 89–101, July–Aug. 1978.

Collins, James C. *Good to Great: Why Some Companies Make the Leap—and Others Don't.* New York: HarperBusiness, 2001.

Collins, James C., and Jerry Porras. *Built to Last.* New York: HarperBusiness, 1994.

Draper's Book of Quotations for the Christian World (Edythe Draper, ed.). Wheaton, Ill.: Tyndale House, 1992.

Earley, Tony. *Jim the Boy.* New York: Little, Brown, 2000.

Farrar, Steve. *Finishing Strong: How a Man Can Go the Distance.* Sisters, Oreg.: Multnomah Books, 1995.

Francis, James Allan. "One Solitary Life." In *The Real Jesus and Other Sermons.* Philadelphia: Judson Press, 1926.

Graves, Stephen, and Thomas Addington. *A Case for Calling: Fulfilling God's Purpose in Your Life at Work.* Nashville, Tenn.: Broadman & Holman, 1998.

Hendricks, Howard. *Values and Virtues.* Sisters, Oreg.: Multnomah Books, 1997.

Hunter, George G., III. *The Celtic Way of Evangelism: How Christianity Can Reach the West—Again.* Nashville, Tenn.: Abingdon Press, 2000.

Junger, Sebastian. *The Perfect Storm: A True Story of Men Against the Sea.* New York: Norton, 1997.

Kouzes, James M., and Barry Z. Posner. *The Leadership Challenge: How to Get Extraordinary Things Done in Organizations.* San Francisco: Jossey-Bass, 1987.

Peters, Thomas J., and Robert H. Waterman, Jr. *In Search of Excellence: Lessons from America's Best-Run Companies.* New York: HarperCollins, 1982.

Pine, Joseph B., II, and James Gilmore. *The Experience Economy: Work Is Theatre and Every Business a Stage.* Boston: Harvard Business School Press, 1999.

Roper, David. *Seeing Through.* Grand Rapids, Mich.: Discovery House, 1997.

Smalley, Gary, and John Trent. *The Two Sides of Love: What Strengthens Affection, Closeness, and Lasting Commitment?* Pomona, Calif.: Focus on the Family, 1990.

Spence, Gerry. *How to Argue and Win Every Time: At Home, at Work, in Court, Everywhere, Every Day.* New York: St. Martin's Press, 1995.

Swindoll, Charles. *Joseph: From Pit to Pinnacle.* Dallas: Insight for Living, 1990.

Swindoll, Charles. *Solomon: Bible Study Guide.* Dallas: Insight for Living, 1998.

Twain, Mark. *Mark Twain's Notebook: Prepared for Publication with Comments by Albert Bigelow Paine.* New York: HarperCollins, 1935.

VanAuken, Sheldon. *A Severe Mercy* (2nd ed.). San Francisco: Harper San Francisco, 1980.

White, Jerry, and Mary White. *Friends and Friendship.* Colorado Springs: NavPress, 1982.

Wilkinson, Bruce. *The Prayer of Jabez.* Sisters, Oreg.: Multnomah Books, 2000.

The Authors

Stephen R. Graves and *Thomas G. Addington* have been business partners and friends for over a decade. For the last twelve years, they have been exploring how to blend business excellence with biblical wisdom through consulting, teaching, mentoring, and writing around the world. This mission statement, originally scratched out on a breakfast napkin early one morning twelve years ago, has been their "never lost" system as they have journeyed through a variety of entrepreneurial endeavors and experiments. They founded Cornerstone Group Consulting and the *Life@Work* journal, they speak regularly in business, ministry, and academic settings, they publish frequently, they serve on national boards, and they are active in coaching leaders toward the finish line. Both hold a doctorate, both are deeply devoted to their families, and both love the never-ending challenge of meshing real life with the message of Jesus.

About Cornerstone Group

For over twelve years, Cornerstone Group has been helping leaders and organizations navigate their way to success. We have provided assistance at every stage of the development bell curve: the exciting, confident "go go" stage; the reflective, cautious "slow go" stage; and the discouraging, confusing "no go" stage. Each stage of organizational life produces its own unique set of challenges and opportunities. Whether you are a small or large nonprofit, a family business going through transition, or a medium-sized company trying to move to the next level, we can provide a valuable helping hand. Our list of clients is impressive; our reputation is rich, and our approach is refreshing.

What We Do Best

- Identify "what's broken"
- Grow business into mass retail
- Construct a compelling future vision
- Align boards and organizations
- Coach leadership transitions
- Advise senior leaders
- Make plans happen
- Create leadership teams
- Expand into international markets

CORNERSTONE GROUP

The Art of Change

Contact us and let us send you a brochure and talk about a free White Board Session (taddington@cornerstoneco.com or (479) 236-0665/ sgraves@cornerstoneco.com or (479) 236-0664).

Index

A

Abortion debate, 52

Absent-Minded Professor, The, 17

Abuse, cases of, 74, 157

Acts 8:22–23, 80

Acts 10, 133

Acts 16, 134

Acts 20:20, 133

Acts, book of, 166

Adaptation of messages, 95–96

Adelphia, 73, 74

Adler, M., 58

Advice and counsel; words of, 2, 56

Advising, defined, 105. *See also* Mentoring

Aesop's fable, 34–35

Affirming, cheerleading and, 125–127

Affirming phase, 113

African proverb, 145

Agenda-setting, 108–109, 169. *See also* Intentionality

Alexander III of Macedon (Alexander the Great), 31

Alexandra, 157, 158

Alpha issues, 109–110

Ambition, 148

America Online (AOL), 48

Amin, I., 10

Andrew, 108, 165

Anonymous proverbs, 31, 129

Antecedent ethos, 42–43, 77

Apathetic, origin of, 65

Apologizing, 82

Applying influence, tools for. *See* Universal tools

Apprenticeship, 104, 105

Archimedes, 117

Argument: lines of, 35–39, 51, 52; and strife, words of, 58

Aristotelian Triangle: elements of, 41–43; embodiment of, 92, 163; incomplete, 72; key link in, 43; personal relevancy of, 43–44. *See also* Ethos; Logos; Pathos

Aristotle's teachings: application of, example of, 39–41; core of, 41–43; cultural factors leading to, 32–33; on the idea of the common place, 52–53, 75; influence of, 31–32; key points on, 45; lines of argument identified in, 35–39, 51, 52; in rhetoric school, 33–35; uniqueness of, 64. *See also* Aristotelian Triangle; Ethos; Logos; Pathos

Arthur Andersen, 74, 86

Artistic proof, basis of, 34

Asking for gifts, 16, 17, 20–21, 22, 128

Athenian culture, 32–33

Complexity, clearing up, 19–20
Confidants, need for, 151
Conflict resolution, avoiding, 153–155
Connecting phase, 113
Conscience in the workplace, 138–139
Consequences: arguments using, 35, 51;
    harmful, producing, 25
Consulting: defined, 105; other players
    in, 67. *See also* Mentoring
Continuity and stability, 20
Cornelius, 133
Cornerstone Group, 67
Corporate culture, 69, 70
Corporate ethos, 86
Corporate organization (org) chart,
    131–132
Corporate scandal, 74, 85
Counsel and advice, words of, 56
Counseling: defined, 105; other players
    in, 67. *See also* Mentoring
Crawdad maneuver, 84
Credibility and integrity, 42, 43, 44, 76.
    See also Ethos
Cultural mix, stirring influence into, 100
Cultural shift, 92–93
Culture: corporate, 69, 70; mainstream,
    100

D
Dark Ages, 104
David, 15, 151, 152, 153
Davis, C., 172
Death, relying on, to resolve life's mis-
    takes, 146, 156–157
Deceit and flattery, words of, 57
Deception, 73–74, 77
Decision making, 80
Defining terms, arguments using, 37, 51
Deming, W. E., 122
Diana, Princess of Wales, 162, 163
Difficult situations, slipping out of, 84
Discernment, 17, 18, 81, 84
Disciples as learners, 95
Discipling, defined, 105. *See also*
    Mentoring
Disney, 68
Disproportionate influence, 55–56
Disillusionment, 28

Dividing topics, arguments using, 38,
    51
Divine mystery: accounting for, 170;
    and human intentionality, 22–25,
    26–27
Dobson, J., 172–173
Doing right, consistently, 85
Doing wrong, knowingly, 153
Double standards, 84
Doublespeak, professional, 83–84
Draper's Book of Quotations for the
    Christian World, 91, 171
Dreams, unrealized and shattered, 3
Duration of mentoring, 108, 109

E
Earley, T., 138
Ecclesiastes 2:15, 79
Ecclesiastes 2:16, 79
Ecclesiastes 2:20, 79
Ecclesiastes 3:11, 79
Ecclesiastes, book of, 28
Egotism, 147, 148
Elephant-like resistance, 70
Elijah, 106
Elisha, 106
E-mailing, risk in, 53–54
Embodying influence, example of. *See*
    Jesus
Emotional persuasion, basis of, 34
Empty words, 60
Encouragement and kindness, words of,
    57
Engaged parents, 137
Engagement, seeking, 64
Engels, F., 8
Enron, 74, 86
Environment, awareness of, 66, 68. *See*
    also Pathos
Ephesians 2:10, 172
Ephesians 4:26, 154
Ephesians 5:19, 80
Erosion of ethos, 83–85
Eternal stalling, 70
Eternity: planting influence for,
    172–173; pondering, 79; question-
    ing, 167
Ethical shortcuts, looking for, 25

World-class influencers. *See* Class-seven influencers

WorldCom, 74

Worship, engaging in real, 80

Written versus spoken communication, 53–54

Wrong, knowingly doing, 153

Wrong words, 57–58

Wrongly applying clout, people that are, 10

Y

Young, A., 123–124

Z

Zacchaeus, 91